INNOVATE!

INNOVATE!

How Great Companies Get Started in Terrible Times

THOMAS A. MEYER

WILEY

John Wiley & Sons, Inc.

Published by John Wiley & Sons, Inc., Hoboken, New Jersey.
Published simultaneously in Canada.

For general information on our other products and services or for technical support,
please contact our Customer Care Department within the United States at (800)
762-2974, outside the United States at (317) 572-3993 or fax (317) 572-4002.

Wiley also publishes its books in a variety of electronic formats. Some content that appears
in print may not be available in electronic books. For more information about Wiley
products, visit our web site at www.wiley.com.

Library of Congress Cataloging-in-Publication Data:

Meyer, Thomas A.
    Innovate! : how great companies get started in terrible times alliances / Thomas
A. Meyer.
        p. cm.
    Includes index.
    ISBN 978-0-470-56058-7 (hardback)
        1. New business enterprises—United States.   2. Financial crises—United States.
I. Title.
    HD62.5.M48 2010
    658.1'10973—dc22

                                                                2010003130

Printed in the United States of America.

10 9 8 7 6 5 4 3 2 1

The power of Innovation is within everybody's reach. The power of creation is reserved for God and women. To Miriam, my beloved wife of 29 years, the most wonderful mother of our eight children, and the only individual who has been by my side through thick and thin. Living with a dreamer means contending with the inevitable nightmares as well. I love you, thank you, and God Bless You.

P.S. I love you Robert, Jonathon, Erika, Alexandra, Ursula, Georgianna, Sophia, and Luke . . . with each child, a new, unique, and wonderful inspiration.

CONTENTS

ACKNOWLEDGMENTS

The Power of Three . . . these are three very special people.

First, I would like to thank Susan McDermott, my Senior Editor at John Wiley & Sons. She was the one who gave me many chances to answer the compelling question: What do people need to know during these terrible times? Thank you for your faith and patience.

Second is Jamey Stegmaier. Without his help, this book would not have happened. Jamey stepped up at a time of need to research, interview, and write the Modern Parallels, discover and compose the Lessons, edit the general content, and refine the page proofs. He is a brilliant young writer whose contributions to the book and persistance to keep me on pace has been nothing short of amazing. Jamey is currently involved with two startups: TypeTribe, an online resource for writers seeking targeted audiences and feedback, and Blank Slate Press, a new St. Louis-based publishing company. He balances those two ventures with his full-time position as the Director of Operations at the Catholic Student Center at Washington University in St. Louis, and writes fiction in his spare time. You can follow Jamey's exploits and insights at www.jameystegmaier.com. Thank you for your contributions and your dedication.

Finally is Father Robert Xavier Albert, a black Catholic priest who has been my secret weapon. He has shown me the power of prayer. Father died the day that Susan informed me Wiley wanted to do the book. Thank you for your love and pray for all of us.

I AM, THEREFORE
I INNOVATE

Innovation is an individual sport. At the heart of each idea is an individual's mind and soul. This mind and soul have developed in a unique way by being exposed to many different variables contributing to their formation. Some of these are genetic, some are environmental, but the sum of the parts of this most intricate process is unique to each person and one of the most profound mysteries of life.

One of the important variables in my formation was my father. He was a Depression kid, a World War II vet, and a gold-watch employee for Western Union Co. He was always thinking and tinkering. A couple of his inventions remain vivid in my memory. The famed lawnmower umbrella was a neighborhood classic. He used an old broken umbrella and fastened it to the lawnmower so that he would be shielded from the sun. Then there was my first hockey stick. When the St. Louis Blues hockey team started in our town, hockey was the craze. A real hockey stick was hard to find, so my father made me one out of some wood scraps.

After working 50 years for Western Union, he spent part of his last year on disability because of a heart condition. My father had lived through many employee retirements at Western Union and had never missed a funeral for the many former employees who died over the years. He was a storeroom manager, not an executive, but every day he would wear a white shirt and tie out of respect for his job.

Then one day, while at the dinner table, the doorbell rang and I ran to the door. A delivery person handed me a package with my father's name on it. I brought it in and he opened it. It was a watch, a parting gift for working 50 years at Western Union. My father was a kind man, a happy man, but that day, I saw a very sad look in his eyes despite the smile on his face. He had worked 50 years for a company and they sent him a watch in the mail.

When I was barely 20 years old, my father passed away. I was away at college at the time and returned home for the funeral. As the family grieved the loss of my father, his funeral would teach me a wonderful lesson regarding the spirit of innovation in tough times.

At the Western Union storeroom my father had managed, there were messenger boys who would deliver telegrams on bicycle. Sometimes a bike would break down and the company would buy a new one. My father would always save the pieces from the old bike in a back room. He would then patiently wait for enough pieces to collect until he had enough parts to build a complete bike. He would give it to a kid in the downtown neighborhood who couldn't afford to buy a bike. Over the 50 years he worked at Western Union, my father constructed and gave away so many secondhand bikes that he lost count.

At his funeral, as I stood by his coffin, I met for the first time more than 50 people who had received their first bike from my father. I realized how many lives and futures he had touched by putting together these innovative "recycles" one piece at a time.

My father managed inventory for a living, but he taught me a profound lesson about innovation: The most valuable type of inventories in life are the ideas that you store in your mind and treasure in your soul.

Thomas Meyer
Chief Innovation Officer
St. Louis University

INTRODUCTION

This book is not about the innovation mind-set, the type of mental behavior necessary to create an environment conducive to innovation. Nor is it about a process, plan, or playbook for innovation. These management guidelines work well in product development and business-planning environments, but innovation is a *talent,* not a *skill.* Innovation is a raw ability that needs space and nurturing. Most importantly, it's an individual exercise, not a groupthink or management committee.

Innovation operates on the quantum level; that is, the smallest but most powerful end of the intellectual spectrum. This is why an apparently insignificant innovation can revolutionize the world for better or worse.

Throughout this book, I explore the powerful sources of innovation and demonstrate through empirical examples how innovation has thrived in terrible economic conditions throughout U.S. history. Innovation has played an important role in improving the state of the economy and will be integral in changing the face of the world as it recovers from the recession that began in September 2008.

During terrible times, innovation becomes more apparent to the casual observer because during the darkness of economic panic, like a lighthouse shining on a lost ship, problems are exposed and innovation begins to emerge.

Innovation is an irrepressible, ever-present force within individuals. It cannot be extinguished in the human spirit. As the speed of change increases due to numerous and disparate variables, innovation will remain the catalytic generator that determines an organization's ability to compete in a volatile environment.

I hope to liberate and inspire you to innovate at the quantum level. Consider this book as a "Get Out of Jail Free" card for your brain. You may be surprised to learn of the many ironic twists and turns that inspired individuals to innovate and change the course of history.

The book is organized in a manner that I hope is easy to follow and explore in any order you wish. To force you into a straight-line progression of knowledge would defeat the whole purpose of the book. I have made each chapter self-contained so that you can finish your train of thought before jumping around to other chapters that catch your eye.

Although innovation can pull people and economies out of tough times, it can also have a negative impact on the masses if implemented with unbridled selfishness. Enjoy your newfound freedom to innovate, but use your new powers with integrity.

Chapter 1

RECESSION

Take a moment to look back on economic history in America through the rose-tinted glasses of innovation. You will see the same history, but with a softer tone and a vision of hope. The story is told with a clear focus on innovation. Once you experience the economic tides of innovation, you will understand the ocean of opportunity in a new light.

Terrible times are no match for innovation. A number of great companies have been started during economic downturns. For the purposes of this book, I limited my criteria for what I call a *great company* to those that have continued operations or brand equity through 2009. This eliminates many great innovations, but nevertheless provides a substantial list of companies for the purposes of demonstrating the powers of innovation.

Before we begin our excursion, let's develop a semantic guide to the evolution of the terminology of terrible times. As America has matured, so has the economic language we use to describe bad economic times.

The softening of the language is an effort to calm and restore the confidence of people, which plays a huge part in the ebbs and flows of the economy.

In the 1700s, the preferred description of terrible times was *panic*. It's a word that describes the frenzied scramble to keep the economy afloat. This term stayed in vogue for a while, but lost ground to the dual terms of *depression* and *recession*. These terms have varying degrees of difference, but describe the same kind of economic disaster. That is, until you precede the word *depression* with the adjective *great*. At that point, you have reached the pinnacle of terrible times terminology.

There can and will only be one period in U.S. history described as the Great Depression (1929–1939). This term should describe the worst of the terrible times. It is the standard by which all terrible times terminology will be compared in the future.

Accordingly, we have retreated to the reliable term *recession*, but have introduced even more palatable, situation-specific expressions such as *oil crisis* or *bursting the dot-com bubble*.

Furthermore, if we must admit that there is a recession, we tend to understate the label in a sort of economic optimism. You might hear terms like *downturn* or *slowdown*. We even find terms that refuse to admit the downward trend, such as a *sideways movement*.

For the purposes of this book, I really don't care what you call it. Whatever term gives you more comfort is the one I recommend, but please understand there is not a dime's bit of difference between them as it relates to innovation.

(*Note*: Unemployment rates weren't calculated by the U.S. Bureau of Labor Statistics prior to 1929. All sections on post-1929 recessions will include that data.)

PANIC OF 1797 (1797–1800)

Sailing back to 1797 allows us to experience the first recession in the United States. America was a new nation back then and this turbulent time wreaked havoc on its young economy. The major culprit was the

Bank of England. The Bank was already reeling from the effects of the French Revolutionary War between England and France. This war had caused deflationary repercussions in England. The bank was tied into American commercial and real estate markets and caused the first major disruptions in America's fledgling economic system.

As the American economy began its first battle with a recession, innovations and start-up companies were flourishing. Of course, this young country needed financial services—specifically, banking and investment assistance—to fund and foster business growth. Two companies would emerge from this recession to create financial forces that would impact the American economy for generations to come.

Great companies that started during this panic include what would eventually become the largest American bank, Chase Manhattan; and the first company to organize an IPO, Alex, Brown & Sons.

DEPRESSION OF 1807 (1807–1814)

In 1807, U.S. President Thomas Jefferson and Congress passed the Embargo Act. This bill barred trade between the United States and other nations. Eventually the bill was proved unenforceable and was repealed in 1808, but not before it had devastated the shipping industry and caused serious stress to the economy. Many people who worked in the shipping industry were unemployed and the businesses associated with the industry were devastated.

Innovation was introduced into industries ranging from publishing to textiles, home appliances, insurance, pottery, and liquor, to name a few.

Great companies that began during the depression of 1807 include John Wiley & Sons, The Hartford, Rogers Orchards, Roper Industries, Bybee Pottery, and Woodford Reserve.

PANIC OF 1819 (1819–1824)

The panic of 1819 is considered the first major financial crisis in American history, and for good reason. After the War of 1812, the U.S. economy saw an enormous and robust expansion. However, as the panic of 1819 began to have its full impact, the United States began to experience a crisis that would be pervasive and damaging. It spanned the areas of real estate, banks, manufacturing, and agriculture. Unemployment rates reached levels never before seen in this young country.

This panic produced giants in the fields of manufacturing, food processing, publishing, and energy.

Great companies that began during the panic of 1819 include William Underwood Company, Consolidated Edison, Fairbanks Morse, and HarperCollins.

PANIC OF 1837 (1837–1843)

The introduction—or rather, *innovation*—of paper currency initially had a devastating effect on the U.S. economy. Speculation was widespread at this time, but the realization that the banks would be circulating paper instead of gold and silver coins created a panic. Confidence in the banking system collapsed and the result was the failure of many banks across the country.

This panic may have frightened the faint of heart, but for innovators this period produced a banner crop of companies that remain today as icons of innovation.

Great companies that started during the panic of 1837 include Procter & Gamble, Tiffany & Co., Berkshire Hathaway, Dun & Bradstreet, Motts, and Stanley.

PANIC OF 1857 (1857–1858)

The failure of the New York branch of the huge Ohio Life Insurance and Trust Company sent shock waves throughout America and Europe. This resulted in a drastic decrease in European speculation for U.S. railroads, consequently crippling many railroad-related businesses and putting great pressure on U.S. banks, which lost consumer confidence. The jobless rate soared all over the United States and brought with it regular protests by laid-off workers. This was the first recession that was fueled by a reactive European influence, and the first to demonstrate the interrelated effects that a world economy can cause.

Nonetheless, new inventions and companies sprouted up across America that would become part of Americana forever. *Great companies* that started in the panic of 1857 include Macy's, Bemis Company, Fifth Third Bank, Cooper Chemical Company, and First Hawaiian Bank.

THE LONG DEPRESSION (1873-1879)

The Long Depression, resulting in a nationwide downturn, was caused by two significant economic events. First, on May 9, 1873, the Vienna Stock Exchange in Austria crashed. This had a crushing effect on the largest American Bank, Jay Cooke & Company in Philadelphia, which eventually declared bankruptcy on September 18, 1873. Second was the adoption of the Coinage Act of 1873, which embraced gold as the standard and demonetized silver. Together, these events had a rippling negative effect through the U.S. economy that lasted seven years.

The Long Depression produced an even longer list of innovators that would build companies that would stand the test of time. *Great companies* that started in the Long Depression include Adolph Coors Company, Barnes & Noble, Cincinnati Bell, Kohler Company, Puget Sound Energy, Ralphs, Zions Bancorporation, ADT Security Services, Bank of America, Pacific Press Publishing Association, R.J. Reynolds Tobacco, Chagrin Falls Popcorn Shop, Conoco Inc., Performance Food Group, Prudential Financial, Stacy Adams Shoe Company, Thomas Organ Company, A. Schwab, BVD, BernzOmatic, Diebold, Eli Lilly and Company, Hendrick Manufacturing Company, Jockey International, Ladenburg Thalmann, Spalding, Bee Group Newspapers, Burpee Seeds, E.W. Scripps Company, F.W. Woolworth Company, Geiger, Menen, Mohawk, St. Louis Refrigerator Car Company, Bankers Life and Casualty, Chattem, Chevron Corporation, General Electric, Inglenook Winery, McNeil Laboratories, I. Magnin, Principal Financial Group, and Scott Paper Company.

PANIC OF 1893 (1893–1896)

Railroads were the speculators' choice of investment in the late 1800s. When they went bad, they had a crippling effect on the economy. The Reading Railroad (yes, it was an actual railroad before the PBS show) of the United States failed, which influenced European investors to withdraw their investments, which in turn crushed the economy.

The broad-based effects of this bankruptcy caused the loss of many jobs, and it also affected the stock market as investors began to pull their money out of the markets. In addition, many banks failed. These major activities also caused a run on gold and incited panic throughout the financial markets.

As you now might suspect, this depression did not keep the innovators down; in fact, many would say this crop of companies might be the sweetest of them all.

Great companies that started in the 1890s recession include IBM; The Hershey Company; Maytag; Weber-Stephen Products Co.; Popular, Inc.; Tootsie Roll Industries; Stags' Leap Winery; Stewart Information Services Corporation; Eckrich; G.R. Kinney Company; Gelco; Cowles Publishing Company; Melville Shoe Corporation; Stromberg-Carlson, Tutor Perini Corporation; DePuy; Elliott Company; Harris Corporation; Lennox International; Lincoln Electric; Malheur Bell; J.C. Newman Cigar Company; Post Foods; Schwinn Bicycle Company; Anchor Brewing Company; Church and Dwight; Macmillan Publishers; New York Telephone; Schmitt Music; T. Marzetti Company; and the Wisconsin Energy Corporation.

PANIC OF 1907 (1907–1908)

The first major financial crisis of the nineteenth century was precipitated by the failure of several Wall Street brokerages and the collapse of the Knickerbocker Trust Company. This resulted in a contracted money supply, which led to the failure of many businesses and financial institutions.

The Cleveland administration worked closely with J.P. Morgan to restore order by channeling money from larger institutions to smaller ones. This crisis led the country to eventually pass financial reforms and establish the Federal Reserve System, an innovation in itself.

The woes of Wall Street had little impact on the surging innovation and entrepreneurial spirit in America at the turn of the century, as demonstrated by the many new ideas and companies that were created during this period.

Great companies that started during the panic of 1907 include Bessemer Trust, Block Drug, Blue Bell Creameries, Böwe Bell & Howell, Dairylea Cooperative Inc., Dr. Scholl's, Dutch Boy, Faygo, Integrys Energy, Leupold & Stevens, Moody National Bank, Neiman Marcus, Praxair, The Hoover Company, UPS, Western Publishing, Briggs and Stratton, Bush Brothers & Company, CIT Group Inc., Converse, Filene's Basement, Fisher Body, General Motors, Harley Ellis Deveraux, Holler House, Pero Vegetable Company, Speed Queen, Williams Companies, and Yale University Press.

POST-WORLD WAR I RECESSION (1918-1922)

The end of World War I brought with it extremely high employment and inflation. This reflected the decrease in manufacturing production that was no longer necessary during peacetime. Not only did people who had jobs during the war lose them, but troops returning from war struggled to find employment as well. This combination drove unemployment to record highs. With no precedent with which to compare, America was unprepared to deal with this confluence of negative factors in the economy.

This adjustment may have caused the increase in the amount of innovative activity that was demonstrated by the many new ideas and companies that sprouted up during this period.

Great companies that were started in the post-World War I recession include A-Treat Bottling Company, AgStar Financial Services, Brookville Equipment Corporation, Celanese, Cowen Group, Dominick's, Houchens

Industries, Peragallo Pipe Organ Company, Ritz Camera Centers, TIAA-CREF, The Timberland Company, Universal Corporation, West Coast Shoe Company, Woodman's Food Market, Zenith Electronics, Allen Family Foods, Boone Drug, Charles of the Ritz, Columbia Pictures, Columbus Tubing, Community Coffee, ConAgra Foods, Cornwell Tools, Cummins, Fanny Farmer, Ferro Corporation, Foster Grant, Great Western Bank, Griffith Laboratories, Haliburton, Hess Corporation, Hilton Hotels, Holdings of American International Group, Jervis B. Webb Company, KitchenAid, Malt-O-Meal Company, Musso & Frank Grill, Ovson Egg, Peter Paul Candy Manufacturing Company, Pioneer Instrument Company, RCA, Red Ball Corporation, Rosendin Electric, Shaw's Star Market, Tandy Corporation, Toro, United Artist, AMC Theatres, Arizona Public Service, Ben Franklin Stores, CR England, Cameron International Corporation, CoorsTek, Dobson Cellular, Dorrance Publishing, and White Castle.

RECESSION OF 1926 (1926–1927)

Arguably the most forgotten recession in the United States because it came before the Great Depression, the recession of 1926 caused much pain to many people as business activity dropped 12.2 percent and trade/industrial activity went down by 10 percent. The recession was caused primarily by labor strikes in Britain and Germany, as well as the widespread effect of Henry Ford halting production for six months to switch over from the Model T to the Model A (innovation can cause recessions just as much as it can pull economies out of them).

This period was a foreshadowing of devastation to come and provided insight on how the world economy was becoming more interdependent.

Even though this period lasted only 13 months, many new companies were born from innovative ideas and inventions. *Great companies* started during the recession of 1926 include Catawissa Bottling Company; Container Corporation of America; Cooper Tire & Rubber Company; Crane Merchandising Systems; David Sunflower Seeds; Haggar Clothing;

Howard Miller Clock Company; IGA Supermarkets; Jel Sert; Maid-Rite; McKinsey & Company; Mt. Olive Pickle Company; NBC; Nationwide Mutual Insurance Company; Nocona Athletic Goods Company; Orange Julius; Oregon Steel Mills; Paul K. Guillow, Inc.; Selective Insurance Group; Spring Air Company; Swiss Colony; Trailways of New York; UAL Corporation; Quick Tires; 7-Eleven; American Family Insurance; Arthur J. Gallagher & Co.; Bali; Blue Bird Corporation; Bonne Bell; Browning Arms Company; CBS; Community Supermarkets; The Derrydale Press; Eaton Harbors Corporation; Fairchild Camera and Instrument; Georgia-Pacific; Gerber Products Company; Growmark; Herberger's; Jays Foods; Kinder Morgan; La-Z-Boy; Marriott International; Mutual Savings Life; Northrop; Oberweis Dairy; Resistol; Ted's Hot Dogs; Theisen's; Zaro's Bakery; Ziff Davis; and Zimmer Holdings.

THE GREAT DEPRESSION (1929-1939)

Unemployment rates: 1929, 3.2 percent; 1933, 24.9 percent; 1939, 17.2 percent.

Starting with the stock market crash on October 29, 1929 (Black Tuesday), the Great Depression would become the largest economic disruption in the history of the world.

Beginning in the stock market, moving to the banks and to agriculture, this period wreaked havoc around the world for a period of nearly 10 years. The global downward spiral would devastate individuals and businesses at an alarming rate.

Most agree that it did not end until the beginning of World War II.

It is a testament to the power of innovation that even during the most terrible depression in U.S. history, hundreds of innovators founded companies that would eventually become world-class corporations.

Great companies started in the Great Depression include Acme Boots; Ampco Pittsburgh; Andronico's; Buehler Food Markets, Inc.; Carvel; First Jersey Credit Union; General Foods; Grumman; Home Federal Banks; Macy's, Inc.; Masco; Mooney Airplane Company;

ServiceMaster; United Technologies; Walter Lantz Productions; AMETEK; Benco Dental; Bendicks; CenturyTel; Dewey's Bakery; Dodge & Cox; Fisher-Price; Geophysical Services Inc.; Markel; Nat Sherman; Parr Lumber; Publix; Rodale, Inc.; Starwood Hotels & Resorts Worldwide; Texas Instruments; Allstate; Baxter International; Clifton's Cafeteria; Estes Express Lines; Giant Eagle; John L. Scott; Marsh Supermarkets; Maurices; Mobil; PerkinElmer; Serta; Sleepy's; Southwest Gas Corporation; Tyson Foods; Zondervan; Advance Auto Parts; Bashas'; Beloit Civic Theatre; Bruno's; Deb Shops; Doeren Mayhew; Ethan Allen; Goodman & Company; Greene Plastics Corp.; High's Dairy Store; Kansas City Steak Company; Krystal; Noble Energy; Mrs. Fisher's, Inc.; Olan Mills; Oriental Trading Company; Pioneer Services; Quil Ceda Leather; Revlon; Rocky Brands, Inc.; Smith's Food and Drug; Toddle House; Willis & Gieger Outfitters; Yarnell Ice Cream Co.; Zippo; ATW Assembly & Test Worldwide; E & J Gallo Winery; Federal Deposit Insurance Corporation; Felpausch; Frankoma Pottery; Giant Foods; Global Partners; Global Van Lines; Gorman-Rupp Company; Guadalupe-Blanco River Authority; Haggen Food & Pharmacy; IC Bus; Knight Ridder; Marvel Entertainment; Mayfran International; Navy Federal Credit Union; Peter Pan Bus Lines; Rockwell Collins; Ryder; Trinity Industries; Waldenbooks; Warner Bros. Cartoons; Amana Corporation; Associated Grocers; DC Comics; East Bay Restaurant Supply; Eimac; Ferguson Company; Gulf+Western; Meijer; Mutual Broadcasting System; Muzak Holdings; Old Dutch Foods; Parker Drilling Company; RaceTrac; Service Merchandise; Steak 'n Shake; Towers Perrin; Zabar's; 20th Century Fox; ADC Telecommunications; Allen Press; Avery Dennison; Beckman Coulter; CUNA Mutual Group; D.A. Davidson & Co.; Friendly's; General Nutrition Centers; Holiday House; Invesco; Leo Burnett; Lucky Stores; Morgan Stanley; Orange Belt Stages; Owens Corning; Penguin Books; Pentagon Federal Credit Union; Perkins and Will; Republic Pictures; Schneider National; Van Dyne Crotty; American Media; Arizona Federal Credit Union; Big Boy; Brooklyn Bottling Group; Gertrude Hawk Chocolates; Glen Glenn Sound; Gordmans; New Directions Publishing; Skidmore, Owings and Merrill; Smithfield Foods;

Stater Bros.; Telex Communications; Trailways Transportation System; Fantasy Publishing Company, Inc.; BHDP Architecture; Brown Derby; Citizens Equity First Credit Union; Colonial Life & Accident Insurance Company; Conlin's Furniture; Dart Container; GEHA; Harrah's Entertainment; Hensel Phelps Construction; Key Food; Krispy Kreme; Osco Drug; Pepperidge Farm; Polaroid Corporation; Red Lion Hotels Corporation; Ritz-Carlton; Sheraton Hotels and Resorts; Stuckey's; T. Rowe Price; Ukrop's Super Market; Academy Sports and Outdoors; Hewlett-Packard; Bridgeport Machines, Inc.; Carlson Companies; Choptank Electric Cooperative; Columbia Sportswear; Cumberland Farms; Dillards; Du-par's; Edlebrock; Guys Snack Foods; Jersey Shore Steel; Kaplan, Inc.; Longs Drugs; Mac Tools; Molex; Pinnacle Entertainment; REI; Restonic Mattress; Science Research Associates; Tractor Supply Company; United Dairy Farmers; Vivitar; Allen Organ; Blue Shield of California; Choice Hotels; Cly-Del Manufacturing; Dollar General; Ferrellgas; Foster Farms; GMAC; Gerber Legendary Blades; Home of Economy; Jack Morton Worldwide; KFC; Marshall Farms; New Albertsons; Roberts Aircraft; Sara Lee Corporation; Schnucks; Vita Craft Corporation; and Wachusett Potato Chip Company.

POST-WORLD WAR II RECESSION (1945)

Unemployment rate: 1.9 percent.

Like its predecessor, World War II created an increased demand in the economy that began to decrease after the conclusion of the war. Certain manufacturers were exclusively dedicated to wartime production, and some could not withstand the unused capacity long enough to evolve to other types of production.

Additionally, the eligible workforce grew substantially as soldiers returned to civilian life and now had to compete for jobs in a contracting economy. This recession was much milder than the previous postwar recession and lasted for a shorter period of time.

Although it lasted only a year, this was sufficient time for a substantial number of innovative companies to rise up.

Great companies that started in the post–World War II recession include Ashley Furniture Industries, Bantam Books, Baskin-Robbins, Cantor Fitzgerald, Circle Line Sightseeing Cruises, Constellation Brands, Do It Best, Factory Motor Parts, Fisher Electronics, Liberty Films, Mattel, Mutual of America, Rich Products, Schreiber Foods, Stewart's Shops, Sub-Zero Refrigerator, U-Haul, United Hardware, and Walter E. Smithe.

LATE 1940s RECESSION (1948–1949)

Unemployment rate: 1948, 3.8 percent; 1949, 6.6 percent.

After the Great Depression, the United States economy settled into a pattern of routine business cycles affected primarily by three factors: interest rates, money supply, and inflation.

The economic balancing act of the Federal Reserve was key in the post–Great Depression economic structure. As in previous recessions, unemployment rates rose to 6 percent as money became tight and businesses began to fail.

By that point, the innovative engine room had established years of counterintuitive results, and this recession was no different.

Great companies that started in the late 1940s recession include Allegran; American State Bank; Atlas Van Lines; Buckle; Bushnell Corporation; Coco's Bakery; Dick's Sporting Goods; Emerson Radio; Gilson Graphics; In-N-Out Burger; Manpower Inc.; Mid-South Management Company Inc.; Oak Manufacturing; Oceana Publications; NVR; Service Electric; Swensen's; Tom Thumb Food & Pharmacy; Toys "R" Us; True Value; Robert Half; Vermeer Company; Winchell's Donuts; World Dryer; 20th Century Fox Television; Adams Cable; ADP; Brown's Chicken & Pasta; Diners Club; Ethicon Inc.; Frontier Oil; Hargray; Hornady; Martinizing Dry Cleaning; Medtronic; Mithun, Inc.; Nabholz Construction; Norms Restaurants; PEMCO; Rowman & Littlefield; Salem Press; Schaper Toys, Skyline Chili; TDIndustries; Taft Broadcasting; United Federal Credit Union; and Winzen Research.

POST-KOREAN WAR RECESSION (1953-1954)

Unemployment rate: 1953, 2.9 percent; 1954, 5 percent.

As we have seen throughout history, post-war periods predictably produce economic recessions. This particular recession was again fueled by the adjustment of wartime manufacturing production, which had brought about a large inflationary period. This came tumbling down after the war, and unemployment rates soared.

The second factor that contributed to this recession was the policy stance of the Federal Reserve. In an attempt to control inflationary pressures, the Fed became more restrictive in its monetary policy, which caused business failures.

By this time, we can see very clearly that recessions are having no negative effect on innovation and entrepreneurship in America; rather, they seem to be encouraging them. The ideas, inventions, and start-ups simply reflect the lifestyles, technological breakthroughs, and consumer needs of the time.

Great companies started in the Post–Korean War recession include Altman Lighting Co., Ann & Hope, Arthur Rutenberg Homes, Banquet Foods, Bill Miller Bar-B-Q, Bob Evans Restaurants, Body Glove, Champion Homes, Chico's Tacos, Claster Television, Colgate-Palmolive, Computer Control, Cruiser Yachts, Denny's, Encore Capital Group, Hamilton, International Speedway Corporation, Koss Corporation, Liberty Lines Transit, Marmon Group, PRO Group, Panavision, Playboy Enterprises, Precision Castparts Corp., Publisher's Clearing House, STP, SafeAmerica Credit Union, Sarasota Coastal Credit Union, Sherwood, Spancrete, Umpqua Holdings Corporation, Walt Disney Studios Motion Pictures, Weston Woods Studios, American Motors, Ameristar Casinos, Ann Taylor, Apache Corp., Bernell Corporation, Bob's Stores, Chateau Ste. Michelle, Commodore International, Handy Hardware, IMS Health, Jerry's Subs & Pizza, Kraco Enterprises, LaRosa's Pizzeria, Lennar Corporation, Mile of Cars, Millipore Corporation, Norris Craft Boats, Putt-Putt Fun Center, Ramada, SCAFCO, Scott's Food & Pharmacy, Shakey's Pizza, and Tasco.

RECESSION OF 1957 (1957-1958)

Unemployment rate: 1957, 4.2 percent; 1958, 6.2 percent.

The recession of 1957 again reflects the power of the Federal Reserve. Due to a tightened money supply, this period experienced many business failures and a high rate of unemployment.

In the modern era, we begin to see the pattern of business cycles and the importance of the role of the Federal Reserve. Whenever the supply of money becomes unbalanced, we see serious economical ebbs and flows. Nonetheless, innovators in this period are not disheartened by the monetary policies as they continue to redefine industries and create more businesses.

Great companies started during the recession of 1957 include Anixter International; Boise Cascade; Bottom Dollar Food; Cavenders; Columbia Helicopters; Curtis Mathes Corporation; Dick Clark Productions; Digital Equipment Corporation; Enterprise Rent-a-Car; Farm Fresh Food & Pharmacy; Food Lion; Hancock Fabrics; Harvey Films; Hyatt; KB Homes; LeSEA; Mirisch Company; Mortgage Guaranty Insurance Corporation; O'Reilly Auto Parts; Powell Industries; Ross Stores; Sizzler; Valentino's; Allied Capital; Beginner Books; Club Car; Cost Plus, Inc.; Datalink Corporation; Filmways; First Alert; First Command Financial Planning, Inc.; GAI Consultants, Inc.; The Gallup Organization; Harriet Carter; Hush Puppies; International Flavors and Fragrances (IFF); The Jim Henson Company; Luxco; Maker's Mark; Monadnock Lifetime Products; Music World Corporation; Pizza Hut; QuikTrip; S&S Cycle; Trader Joe's; VIP Parts, Tires and Service; Village Inn; and Walmex.

RECESSION OF 1960 (1960-1961)

Unemployment rate: 1960, 5.2 percent; 1961, 6 percent.

The recession of 1960 began with the introduction of a new term referring to the average person's perspective on businesses that affect his or her life: *consumer confidence*. The lack of consumer confidence in U.S.

banks and overall government caused a devastating impact on business, resulting in numerous bankruptcies. This caused higher unemployment and increased inflation.

President Kennedy's urging to increase government spending ultimately improved the gross domestic product (GDP, the measure of the number of goods and services produced in America within a year), reducing unemployment and improving consumer confidence.

Innovators had their own kind of confidence and as usual took things into their own hands. This resulted in new technologies and businesses.

Great companies started in the recession of 1960 included Domino's Pizza; Duane Reade; Eastpak; Fry's Food and Drug; Gate Petroleum; Golden West Books; Heatter-Quigley Productions; IBP, Inc.; Institute of Scientific Information; Interpublic Group of Companies; Kimco Realty Corporation; Let's Go Travel Guides; Plaid Pantry; Redken; Rural King Supply; Rutherford & Chekene; Sabre Holdings; Sea-Land Service; Sealed Air; Semtech; Taco Time; Tower Records; Tyco International; Vitamin World; Wausau Homes, Inc.; Aero Union; Amrep Corporation; Beasley Broadcast Group; Burgerville, USA; Creare, Inc.; David Bruce Winery; Eagle Insurance; Great Lakes Theatre Festival; Heitz Wine Cellars; Humana; K2 Sports; Lutron; Mazzio's; Memorex; Mercury Insurance; Papa Gino's; Rysher Entertainment; Six Flags; Strat-O-Matic; Taco Tico; Time-Life; Wienerschnitzel; and Winegardner and Hammons.

RECESSION OF 1969 (1969–1970)

Unemployment rate: 1969, 3.4 percent; 1970, 6.1 percent.

This economic downturn was relatively mild compared to previous recessions, but the telltale signs of high unemployment and rising inflation were there.

This period also ushered in more sophisticated models of economic forecasting. The U.S. government and Federal Reserve improved their response rates to avoid another Great Depression.

All of this had minimal bearing on the surge in innovation and entrepreneurial activity, as these forces were stronger than ever.

Great companies started during the recession of 1969 include Acxiom; Advanced Micro Devices; AlphaGraphics; Arbor House; Captain D's; The Children's Place; Coaxial Dymanics; CompuServe; DST Systems; Danaher Corporation; Dataprobe; Doubletree; ENSCO, Inc.; Equity Residential; Fortune Brands; Gap; Ground Round; IDX Systems; Investors Bank & Trust; Key Tronic; KinderCare Learning Centers; Korn/Ferry; Little Tikes; Long John Silver's; MTM Enterprises; Mayfield Fund; Mentor Corporation; Micro Instrumentation and Telemetry Systems; Miller-Boyett Productions; Mountain Safety Research; The Old Spaghetti Factory; Love Cosmetics; Penske Corporation; ROLM; Raines International; Red Robin; Refco; Science Applications International Corporation; Skipper's; SofTech; Spelling Television; Stew Leonard's; SureFire; Sysco; Telephone and Data Systems; Verbatim Corporation; Watermark; Wendy's; ANSYS, Inc.; American National Carbide; Andrews McMeel Universal; Aquarius Records; Bomanite; Boston Properties; Bresslergroup; Celestial Seasonings; David R. Godine; Days Inn; Dialcom; Edmark; FedEx Office; Flying Buffalo; Hollandia Produce; ISACOMM; Innovis; Jones Apparel Group; LXD Incorporated; Last Gasp; Mr. Tire; National Safety Associates; Paladin Press; Prince Sports; Redner's Markets; STX; Saatchi & Saatchi; Schnake Turnbo Frank; System Planning Corporation; Urban Outfitters; Western Digital; and the Yankee Group.

OIL CRISIS OF 1973 (1973–1975)

Unemployment rate: 1973, 4.9 percent; 1975, 8.2 percent.

American ingenuity meets Middle East oil. The oil crisis of 1973 ushered in an age of energy economics and the effect it would have on the world economy for years to come. The United States and much of the world was now dependent on oil for the functions of business and everyday life.

Middle Eastern countries were empowered by an economic bargaining chip at the world's expense and began to play it to their advantage. The sharp increase in price and shortage in supply had an immediate and damaging effect on the U.S. economy. It was also a major wake-up call to the automotive industry as this crisis became evident to anyone who had to fill their tank with gas. It was common to wait in line for gas or to see a gas station temporarily out of gas.

Innovators and entrepreneurs saw this crisis as just another speed bump in the road of life, and it had little effect on new technologies and companies.

Great companies started during the oil crisis of 1973 include Alcalde & Fay; Alice James Books; Apollo Group; Asian America Theater Company; Bain & Company; Cablevision; Cobra Golf; Compuware; Depository Trust & Clearing Corporation; Freese-Notis; Game Designer's Workshop; George Street Co-op; Golden Corral; Gremlin Industries; Griggstown Quail Farm; Honey Dew Donuts; Hungry Howie's Pizza; Institute for International Research; International Quality and Productivity Center; Kicker; Louisiana-Pacific; MBIA; MGM Home Entertainment; New Harbinger Publications; No Nonsense; Nylink; Olivia; PSI Seminars; Price Chopper; RE/MAX; Ramsey Corporation; Rockford Fosgate; SuperStock; TSR, Inc.; Trading Places International; Weaver Leather; Winston Airport Shuttle; Arbor Drugs; Benshaw; Burke Corporation; Digital Research; William Drake; E-One; Foot Locker; Furniture Row; Gemini Sound Products; Gentex; Hampton Jitney; Harvest House; JAM Creations; Jameco Electronics; Kendall-Jackson; Knights Inn; Landmark Theatres; Laserfiche; Mellow Mushroom; Mongoose; Osprey Packs; Rainbow Sandals; Resort Condominiums (RCI); Scurlock Publishing; Shubb; Specialized Bicycle Components; Stave Puzzles; Tandem Computers; Taylor Guitars; Tech Data; Viacom Productions; WMS Industries; AIMCO; Airflow Sciences Corporation; Brinker International; CBM Engineers; Chocolate City Records; Cinematronics; Creative Artists Agency; DuBiel Arms Company; Famous Amos; GOODE Ski Technologies; GTCO; JL Audio; Lawson Software; Maximus; Microsoft, Molecular Probes; Oakley, Inc.; Orion Telescopes & Binoculars; Oxford Analytica; Scentura; Supercuts; TeleVideo; Tellabs; and Turner Sports.

RECESSION OF 1980 (1980–1982)

Unemployment rate: 1980, 6.3 percent; 1982, 10.8 percent.

World oil prices and a tight monetary policy combined to have a devastating effect on the economy in 1980. High prices and high interest rates produced high unemployment. The economy was in turmoil.

This resulted in a change in the monetary policy, but did not prevent some very difficult years in the economy. Many businesses closed, causing unemployment to soar.

When the going gets tough, innovators get going like never before, and this recession had the results to prove it.

Great companies that started during the recession of 1980 include All My Sons Moving; American Technology Corporation; Amgen; Applebee's; Aqua Flow; Ardence; Ashton-Tate; BMC Software; Beagle Bros; British Knights; CQG; Central Point Software; Davie Brown Entertainment; Emmis Communications; Exergen Corporation; FINEX Management Serves; Fuddruckers; Gentle Giant Moving Company; Gyrodata; Harman International Industries; Herbalife; HobbyTown USA; Institutional Venture Partners; Iomega; Krell Industries; Lam Research; Lodgenet Interactive; Maui Jim; Natural Alternatives International; Odwalla; Opus One Winery; Overland Storage; Pacific Data Images; Passport Designs; SL Green Realty; SYNNEX Corporation; Sanmina-SCI Corporation; Scottrade; Second Wind; Serena Software; Steve Jackson Games; Sunbow Productions; Taschen; The Learning Company; Thor Industries; Unison Industries; Valero Energy Corporation; Visibility Corp.; Westell; World Events Productions; AES Corporation; APC by Schneider Electric; Adaptec; Alerton; Amblin Entertainment; American Historic Inns; Andrew Marc; Applied Biosystems; Arthrex; Artisan Entertainment; Aspen Technology; Bitstream Inc.; Blackbaud; Candie's; Carsey-Werner Productions; Chiron Corporation; Cirrus Logic; Collegiate Licensing Company; Comverse Technology; Diskeeper Corporation; ESI International; Eureka Springs and North Arkansas Railway; FlightView; Free Fall Associates; Genzyme; Guess; Halloween Adventure Stores; Harvest Partners; Hunter Industries; Image Entertainment; Impact

Confections; Islands; Jasculca Terman; Kaiser Associates; Kensington Computer Products Group; Kimpton Hotels & Restaurant Group; Kramer Electronics; LSI Corporation; LabVantage Solutions; Labtec; Maxtor; Mentor Graphics; Merrell; Millstone Coffee; PageNet; Paws, Inc.; Quiznos; Rhino Foods; Rocky Mountain Chocolate Factory; Softdisk; Sunrise Senior Living; TCBY; Trivest; United States Satellite Broadcasting; Universal Avionics; Veronis Suhler Stevenson; Vicor Corporation; Wyse; ZymoGenetics; 99 Cents Only Stores; ABC Supply; AMR Corporation; AMS Pictures; AMX LLC; Adobe Systems; Aerostich; Airgas; Amdocs; Autodesk; Barrett Firearms Manufacturing; Bristol Farms; Buffalo Wild Wings; Compaq; Dave & Buster's; Digital Systems Resources; Directed Electronics, Inc.; Great Clips; Green Hills Software; HarbourVest Partners; Huntsman Corporation; Integral Systems; Intertex; JD Squared; JVA Artists; Jackson Hewlitt; Jordan Company; Kole Imports; Landmark Graphics Corporation; Larry's Giant Subs; Lazy Acres; Locus Computing Corporations; Lotus Software; LucasArts; MBNA; Malibu Boats; MicroProse Software; Newman's Own; Olive Garden; Ollie's Bargain Outlet; Opening Day Partners; PC Connection; Panda Energy International; The Princeton Review; Quarterdeck Office Systems; Quintiles; RCTV International; Regency Enterprises; Rule Broadcast Systems; SM&A; Safra National Bank of New York; Scaled Composites; Shawmut Design and Construction; Smith Breeden; Softshare; Sun Microsystems; Sunrider; Symantec; THX; TeleTech; Toth Brand Imaging; TriStar Pictures; Ultimate Play the Game; UltraCade; Vera Bradley; Vertical Communications; and Wasatch Computer Technology.

RECESSION OF 1990 (1990)

Unemployment rate: 6.3 percent.

Many disparate financial factors were at play during this mini recession. This may be why it lasted such a short period of time. The key factor that sent the market south revolved around the collapse of many savings and loan institutions around the country. This caused panic, which brought about a host of negative effects of recession;

specifically, tighter money, loss of businesses, and increased unemployment rates. As the economy slowed, innovators pressed forward with new ideas and new technologies.

Great companies started during the recession of 1990 include ABC Family Worldwide, Inc.; ABI Research; All Media Guide; Amoeba Music; Ariat; AudioFile; Bath & Body Works; Boss Hoss; Champion Ballroom Academy; China Coast; CleveMed; Cogent Inc.; Cooper Firearms of Montana; Delta Tao Software; Distributed Art Publishers; Dollar-Thrifty Automotive Group; Eagle East Aviation; Ectaco; Empyrean Brewing Company; Farr Associates; Fuji Food; GTE Interactive Media; Hollywood Pictures; Hoover's; IDT Corp.; Icos; Ideal Homes; Ironstone Vineyards; Jamba Juice; Leading Authorities; Nautilus Entertainment Design; Open City; Quacquarelli Symonds; Rambus; Raven Software; Sacks & Co.; Sapient; Library Video Company; Shore Fire Media; Sky Mall; Specter Werkes/Sports; Spyglass, Inc.; Sullivan & Company; Trim Tabs Investment Research; United Electronic Industries; Universal Studios Florida; Vicarious Visions; WayForward Technologies; Wizards of the Coast; Xybernaut; The 3DO Company; ARIAD Pharmaceuticals; Aberdeen LLC; The Allen Group; Amblimaton; Applied Media Technologies; Aricent; Art Technology Group; Aviation Partners; Blizzard Entertainment; Brighton Collectibles; Bristol Technology, Inc.; Broadcom; Bungie; Calera Capital; Candlewick Press; Charlesbank Capital Partners; Corelis; eShop; Epic Games; Everest Group; Flying Edge; Game-House; HSU Research; Hall & Partners; Hammes Company; Hotels.com; Hyland Software; IVI Publishing; id Software; J.G. Wentworth; Kel-Tec; Lee & Low Books; Lexmark; LOG-NET; Manga Entertainment; MoSys, Inc.; Muze; NeuroDimension; New Regency Productions; New York Model Management; Nickelodeon Animation Studios; October Films; Physicians Group Management Services; Premiere Global Services; Proxicom; RF Micro Devices; Renaissance Capital LLC; Seattle's Best Coffee; Sew Fast Sew Easy; Shiekh Shoes; SonicWall; Structuretec; Stu Segall Productions; TCW/ Crescent Mezzanine; Telerama; The Heavyweights, Inc.; Trailer Bridge; Vvi; Warner Bros. Studio Store; and White Wolf.

RECESSION OF 2001 (2001)

Unemployment rate: 5.7 percent.

A toxic combination of terrorist attacks, a technology bust, and a series of corporate accounting scams brought about the recession of 2001 and wreaked havoc on the economy. Many businesses failed, people stopped spending money, and the vicious cycle of a recession was in play. The unusual and tragic events were unique to America and managed to rally many people during this economic downturn.

The dot-com bubble may have burst, but many more innovations were still occurring and new companies were springing up across the country.

Great companies started during the recession of 2001 include 3Dsolve; A123Systems; Accelrys; Activision Value; Acuity Brands; Aeluros Inc.; Albright Group; Animax Entertaiment; Anybots; Architel; Artificial Studios; Ascentium; AsiaPac International; Atom Entertainment; BMI Gaming; Barking Lizards Technologies; Beat the Traffic; BizChair.com; Buzz Monkey Software; CRG West; Casemate Publishers; Cavium Networks; Chicago Gaming; Chronic Logic; Cobraguard; Collaborative Fusion; Cordiem; Cortina Systems; Dabel Brothers Productions; Dalberg Global Development Advisors; Devicescape Software; Digital Eel; Digital Trends; eFileCabinet; EcoDuro; Eos Press; FBM Software; First Equity Card Corporation; Fuchsia; Funambol; GameSoft Publishing; Gratis Internet; GreatBigStuff; Heritage Web Solutions; Integrated Broadband Services; Ionian Technologies; J.C. Flowers; Johnny Cupcakes; July Systems; Kaleidescape; Konarka Technologies; Large Animal Games; Legend Films; Lithium Technologies; Live Oak Brewing Company; M2SYS Technology; MDS America; Matrix Games; Mark Logic; Maxum Games; Medix Staffing Solutions; Minecode; Mirant; Moe's Southwest Grill; Mondo Times; Motricity; MumboJumbo; Newegg; One Equity Partners; Peppercoin; PeriShip; Pillar Data Systems; Plexifilm; Prime Healthcare Services; Pureology; Raw Thrills; ResellerRatings; Rivet Software; Rocketplane Limited, Inc.; SMS.ac, Inc.; Santa Cruz Games; Saratoga Technologies; Screenlife; SelectSoft Publishing; SigmaQuest; Simplicato; Six Apart; Ska Studios; Sparkfactor

Design; Speck; Stratavia; TerraCycle; Three Rings Design; Total Phase; TriGeo Network Security; Tuvox; Twisted Oak Winery; US-Mattress; UnitedLayer; Viper Comics; VoiceBox Technologies; Wahoo Studios; Westpark Foundries; Xnergy; Zoom Corporation; Zuffa; and Zultys.

RECESSION OF 2008 (2008–TBD)

Unemployment rate: 2008, 4.9 percent; September 2009, 9.8 percent.

As this book is written in 2009, the economic crisis that began in 2007 persists. The devastative effects of high unemployment and contraction of credit are spread across multiple industries, including real estate, banking and financial services, manufacturing, and retail.

However, as history has certainly taught us, this will be a time of great innovation and entrepreneurial endeavors despite the viewpoint that this is an impossible time to start a business or create a new product or service. I hope this short economic history tour has given you hope and demonstrates that downtimes are no match for innovation.

Chapter 2

PERSEVERANCE

Thomas A. Edison
General Electric Company

There is no other person or company that captures the power of perseverance as effectively or as thoroughly as Thomas Alva Edison and the General Electric Company. Over the next several pages I highlight what inspired Edison to innovate, invent, and industrialize many life-changing innovations.

Edison was the last of seven children and did not learn to talk until he was four years old. This silence was offset by an unending source of curiosity that remained with him for the remainder of his life.

In his early childhood, Edison was an inquisitive child who relentlessly questioned his teachers in school. In today's society, Edison would have most certainly been diagnosed with attention deficit hyperactivity disorder. One teacher even ridiculed him for his constant curiosity. This convinced his mother to withdraw the young boy from school at age seven and to teach him at home. She was convinced that he was a remarkably intelligent child.

The remainder of Edison's childhood learning experience was fulfilled by a homeschooling program under his mother's tutelage that concentrated on the basic subjects of reading, writing, arithmetic, and the Bible. His father introduced him to the great classics in literature.

As Edison reached the ripe old age of eleven, his mother took him to the library for the first time. His love for self-learning soared as he discovered a world of knowledge on virtually every subject. Soon, he had devoured volumes of books at an incredible pace. His love for science and his natural curiosity grew exponentially as he continued his quest for knowledge.

THE LESSON: THE POWER OF CURIOSITY

Curiosity is a trait that you will see mentioned throughout this book. Everyone is born with a curious nature; this is the method by which the unformed brain learns how the world works, and how it works in relation to the world. The key as you age is to nurture this curiosity so you continue to grow and challenge yourself to improve your life. Live without intellectual restraints. The part of the brain that controls risky behavior and thinking skills isn't fully developed until around age 25, so if you want to wire your brain to think outside of the box on a daily basis, you have a limited time to do so.

■ ■ ■

Two interesting personal qualities developed in the young Edison that would serve him well for the rest of his life. The first was his courage to question everything. This independent thinking was a major factor in his success as an inventor. The second quality was his disdain for highbrow language. He preferred the language of the common man and saw little value in a pretentious intellectual vocabulary. This desire to communicate on the level of common people greatly assisted him in industrializing his ingenious inventions.

THE LESSON: THE POWER OF COMMUNICATION

After all, if you can't communicate your ideas, what good are they? Whether you're pitching your idea to a billionaire investor or to your first potential client, you need to be able to explain your innovation in a clear, concise manner. Avoiding unnecessarily highbrow language gives you access to millions more people than if you can only explain your idea in a purely technical manner. Without their ability to explain the most complex concepts in the universe in the common tongue, Stephen Jay Gould, Stephen Hawking, Oliver Sachs, and Brian Greene may have just been brilliant scientists instead of *best-selling* brilliant scientists.

When Edison reached the age of 12, he had the mental capacity of a grown man. He was ready to begin his adult life, and so he ventured into the produce and publishing worlds . . . well, sort of. He began selling papers, fruits, and snacks on the local railroad. Eventually he borrowed the information coming over the teletype machines at the railroad stations to create his own little newspaper, the *Weekly Herald*.

■ ■ ■

While peddling his newspaper on the train route, Edison angered one of the conductors, who proceeded to hit him on the side of his head. This blow caused damage to his ear, which had already lost some of its function. Eventually, Edison would lose all of his hearing in his left ear and nearly 80 percent in the right. The lesson: Don't steal information and profit from it. You may not have your ears boxed, but the penalty might be much worse.

Later, Edison learned Morse code and how to use the telegraph. This was the state-of-the-art communication skill of the day. His new-found skill was immediately put to use, and as he turned 15, he took a job as a telegraph operator to replace someone who had to leave for the Civil War. This gave him the opportunity to increase his speed at operating the telegraph, but more importantly it provided him a platform to question how he could improve the device.

He eventually left this job and began a series of failed entrepreneur-ial activities. Discouraged, he returned home to help his ailing parents, particularly his mother. An undiagnosed onslaught of Alzheimer's had rendered her an infant in an adult's body. Edison quickly realized that financial support of his parents was a priority and found a new job at Western Union in Boston.

Western Union and the city of Boston were the perfect combination, as the company provided him with a useful application of his skills as a telegraph operator. More importantly, the city was a hub of the scien-tific and cultural universe of the time. As young Edison come to realize, *location* was as just as important as *occupation* for a successful innovator.

The late nineteenth century was in many ways an early version of the technology boom in Silicon Valley in the 1990s. The preferred method of communication between innovative hotshots was Morse code instead of the Internet, but both involved a network of innova-tors who communicated on a regular basis. Edison was a key member of the club. The current concept of moonlight entrepreneurialism was nothing new for this young group of nineteenth-century techies.

Terrible times call for great innovation; terrible jobs call for inspired moonlighting. Granted, Edison could have had it worse. He could have had no job at all, no source of income. The key was that he found the energy after work to come home and innovate.

THE LESSON: FOUR TIPS FOR A SUCCESSFUL MOONLIGHTER

1. *Keep your day job.* No matter how brilliant your innovation is, you need a way to pay the bills until your idea catches on. Not only should you not quit your day job but you need to give it the time and attention it deserves so your boss lets you continue working there.
2. *Take notes.* You've heard the advice that you should always have a notepad ready for when that million-dollar idea strikes. But how many people actually follow that advice? Fortunately, there are many digital iterations of the old spiral notepad available in the twenty-first century, the most readily available example being

your phone. When that idea strikes, record it in some way. It's not worth losing it.

3. *Turn off the TV.* After a long day of work at an exhausting job, the easiest thing to do is plop down in front of the television, turn on a sitcom, and turn off your brain. Millions of people do this. Do you want to be one of them?

4. *Find a company that encourages moonlighting.* In 2009, we're living in the Innovation Nation. Companies are starting to realize that the happiest and most productive employees are those who are given the freedom to innovate on the job. They break down the barrier between work and moonlighting. The famous example is that Google gives its engineers 20 percent of their time to work on personal projects (projects that are owned by Google). That 20 percent has spawned major components of Google's business, including Gmail and Google News.

■ ■ ■

In this period of 12-hour workdays and serious innovative moonlighting, Edison conceived and applied for his first patent. This patent would teach him the importance of marketing and timing. The invention was an innovative way to cast votes electronically so that results could be immediately calculated without postponing a transition of power. To Edison's surprise, this effective technology was completely rejected by the Massachusetts legislature because it worked too efficiently. It did not meet with approval because the normal delay in voting gave the minority opposition valuable time to create an effective counterattack.

This lesson of market acceptability was not lost on the young innovator. In fact, he vowed never to invent anything again without first gauging the market acceptance of the idea. His first invention worked flawlessly and provided the exact service that was intended, but unfortunately the politicians had viewed it as a threat to the status quo. This realization provided a turning point for Edison to become an innovative businessman, which would serve him well for the remainder of his illustrious career.

MODERN PARALLEL: RANDY COPELAND, VELOCITY MICRO

The year was 1992, and computers were just too slow for Randy Copeland.

Copeland owned a cabinet-making business in Richmond, Virginia. He returned from the field each day with batches of notes and measurements, excited to design the perfect cabinets for his clients. He would start up the 3D modeling software on his desktop computer, load the specs . . . and wait.

Computers of the day were simply too slow for complex software like the kind that Copeland needed. So instead of waiting for the next generation of computers to come out, Copeland—an avid techie—built one of his own in his kitchen.

The resulting computer worked so well that he built another for his company, then another. Soon word got out about his ultra-performance systems stocked with premium hardware, and friends and family members wanted computers of their own. It was as if Copeland was not only letting them glimpse the future of computing power, but he was also letting them live in that future.

Seeing the potential of turning his hobby into a business, Copeland decided to take a page from Edison and moonlight. While maintaining his primary business, he built and sold computers on the side, all the while extending his reach by teaching himself HTML and building the first version of VelocityMicro.com.

Despite being accessible via the web site, by 2001 Copeland was still selling computers mostly to people he knew. He started to doubt the growth potential and relegated his future customers to friends and family.

Then, just a few days before Thanksgiving 2001, Copeland had a breakthrough. He was approached by *Maximum PC* magazine to assemble a PC for their "Boutique PC Roundup." He accepted immediately and then scrambled to research and build a PC over the long weekend.

The review that hit the newsstands in February 2002 reached a few thousand subscribers, but just as importantly, it made Copeland realize that he had a viable product for a broader market. The review noted that the Velocity Micro PC was "put together with the kind of care and craftsmanship the behemoth manufacturers can't offer." Reading the review was a light bulb moment for Copeland. "I can do something with this," he thought.

He soon assembled a small sales and Web team, encouraging them to use the *Maximum PC* review as leverage. They pushed for national exposure and recognition, and they quickly found that there was a specific audience for their niche market beyond those needing to run memory-burning software for their jobs: gamers. Soon gaming magazines across the country were raving about Velocity Micro quality and performance.

Propelled by the strength of those reviews, Velocity Micro's popularity exploded, doubling in size each year over the next few years. In 2005 it began selling in Best Buy stores across the country, further expanding its reach.

Although Copeland maintained the company's focus on high-powered, high-end products, he recognized the need for a more diversified paradigm when the U.S. economy tanked in fall 2008. Within a few months, his team had created the exact opposite of a powerful desktop PC: a small, light, inexpensive netbook geared toward those who used their computers for Internet and travel and not much else. It was the perfect complement to the Velocity Micro product line.

Randy Copeland and Velocity Micro are the epitome of innovation in tough times, whether those tough times are for 3D modelers or gamers tired of waiting for their programs to load or the tough economic times that affect millions across America. From his kitchen in 1992 to the new headquarters in 2009, Copeland exhibited the perseverance necessary to make Velocity Micro the biggest boutique PC producer in North America.

During his relatively short tenure in Boston, Edison was exposed to the value of proximity to talent at the local universities. He spent most of his time at Boston Tech, which would later rebrand itself as MIT and remain one of the premier technology centers of the world. He attended numerous lectures, during which professors discussed the value of *multiplexing* telegraph signals.

The theory behind multiplexing was that the transmission of electrical impulses at different frequencies over telegraph wires could produce simulations of the human voice and even vague images. This was possible by sending the frequencies through a device called the *harmonic telegraph*. (Another bright young guy named Alexander Graham Bell, who was also living in Boston at the time, shared equal enthusiasm for this intriguing theory.) The basic theory led to the invention of the first *articulating* telephone, the first fax machine, and the first microphone.

Through his network of innovative brethren, Edison met Benjamin Bredding, who had already patented a device called a *duplex telegraph line*. This invention took advantage of the electromagnetism relationship and the number and direction of wire windings associated with a connection between telegraph keys, which can influence the current that flows between them. This facilitated two-way communication. Unfortunately, Bredding had a less than honorable business partner who sold the patent out from under Bredding to Western Union without compensating him a single dime.

The unjust treatment of Bredding inspired Edison to enter the world of intellectual property and entrepreneurialism with a keen eye to filter out shady business partners and greedy parasites. Eventually, Edison would be granted a patent for the first quadruplex transmitter—a fellow innovator's tribute to his friend Bredding.

Edison's moonlighting activity was wearing thin at Western Union, a company not known for its entrepreneurial culture (see Introduction) and which was on the verge of giving Edison a pink slip for his lack of focus on the job. Edison felt the pressure and decided to leave before the company dismissal arrived. He borrowed some money from his buddy Benjamin Bredding and took off for New York City, hoping to take advantage of the bustling business environment there.

THE LESSON: GO TO WHERE THE BUSINESS IS

Edison's arrival in New York was less than glorious for the budding innovative entrepreneur, as he had difficulty finding work. While sleeping in empty buildings and without money for food, he became rather desperate for employment. Begging was not something Edison was accustomed to, and the stress of failure was building by the moment.

What happened next not only changed the fortunes of Edison but also helped change the course of history. In his search for employment, Edison had begun to wander into random office buildings, hoping to find work that would fit his talents of electrical knowledge. As he arrived at one particular building that housed a brokerage firm, the office personnel seemed critically concerned over a failure of a stock ticker. The crowd surrounding this equipment had no electrical knowledge and seemed to be in complete panic. Young Edison volunteered to take a look at the ticker; much to everybody's amazement, he fixed it on the spot.

Seeing the potential of this young lad, the office manager hired Edison on a full-time basis to keep the office running. To his surprise, Edison was now making more money than he had ever made at Western Union. But what affected him most was the euphoric feeling of being rescued from the failure and pain of abject poverty. In addition, and most importantly, he could resume his first love of innovative moonlighting.

THE LESSON: CREATE YOUR OWN LUCK

Note the factors that resulted in Edison's turn from helpless poverty to empowered innovator: *persistence*, *initiative*, and *luck*. Luck doesn't just happen to some people and not to others. You have to give yourself ample opportunities to create your own luck. Edison could have wandered the streets of New York waiting for someone to miraculously recognize his brilliance, but instead he persistently visited centers of commerce and took initiative when opportunity arose.

Edison soon established a base of stability and a moonlighting platform that would serve him well. It did not take him long to perfect several inventions, including the quadruplex transmitter and the stock ticker. The financial reward soon followed as he sold his patents for handsome payments that exceeded his wildest imagination. His financial good fortune allowed him to pay back his good friend Bredding and to send his parents enough money to take care of their expenses.

■ ■ ■

This was the beginning of the Edison freight train of innovation. Once his fertile mind was free of the restraints of immediate financial obligations, he became a development dynamo that would impact the world for generations to come. Notably during this time he opened his first laboratory in 1874 in Newark, New Jersey, with the proceeds he had received from various patents. This period was interesting because Edison and Alexander Graham Bell were fierce competitors. It certainly conjures up the image of Bill Gates and Steve Jobs nearly a century later. In fact, Edison's work on the carbon transmitter actually enabled Bell to develop the articulating phone for practical use. It was an intensely competitive time in the electronic and telecommunication fields, and Edison and Bell were striving to create many of the same devices.

THE LESSON: THE POWER OF COMPETITION

Competition creates environments ripe for innovation. Competition adds a sense of urgency to the product development process. It also spurs the innovator to strive for quality and overall utility. Acknowledging your competitors and distinguishing your product from theirs— or figuring out a way to sell it better—leads to successful, lasting innovation.

In 1876, Edison moved his laboratory to Menlo Park, New Jersey. This would become one of the most famous laboratories in the world.

Shortly after his relocation he invented the phonograph in 1877 and the first commercially practical incandescent light bulb in 1879.

■ ■ ■

By 1884, Edison was a frequent contributor to the patent office, but what came next changed the world forever. Edison introduced the world's first economically viable system of centrally generating and distributing electric light, heat, and power. This incredible accomplishment may never be surpassed in the vast world of technology. Never again would he shiver in the corners of abandoned buildings at night as he did when he first moved to New York. His innovation for electric heat would warm his hands—and the world.

What made Edison special? Surely there were other young, bright people in his day who had shivered their way to sleep; other inventors, even. Several other inventors were working on electricity at the same time as Edison: Elihu Thomson, Frank Sprague, and Nikola Tesla. Why did Edison succeed where they had failed? Why is he so famous today, whereas the names of his competing peers are mere fodder for Jeopardy questions?

The truth lies in a combination of four factors:

1. *He read.* Edison didn't just read the classics; he also read technical and scientific literature such as Michael Faraday's *Experimental Researches in Electricity*. Reading relevant trade periodicals kept him up to date on technological advances and also sparked ideas of his own.
2. *He tinkered.* Edison was a consummate tinkerer. When he was a telegrapher early on in life, he took apart the batteries that charged the machines and examined them for the purposes of understanding and improving them.
3. *He cross-fertilized.* Edison always worked on multiple projects at once. Although he embarked on seemingly unrelated projects at the same time—like a new telephone receiver, a method for ore separation, and the electric light—he often found ways that the various ideas

were interconnected. In short, he maximized the possibilities his brain had to make connections that otherwise would not be made.

4. *He delegated.* We picture Edison in a tiny laboratory working by himself into the dead of the night until he finally invented the electric light. In truth, he had a team of researchers and scientists at his disposal and state-of-the-art facilities at Menlo Park in which to work. Without hiring the right people and delegating to them, Edison may not have created the first electrical power plants.[1]

It took the perseverance to combine all four factors to make Edison as successful as he was. If you're looking to be as innovative an inventor as him, you'll need to employ all four as well.

Edison's pioneering brilliance in creating the first form of an electric grid led to the world's first and largest full-scale research and development center in West Orange, New Jersey. This state-of-the-art facility would further establish the electronic age and facilitate more Edison inventions, including the Vitascope, which would lead to the first silent motion picture. In 1892, his Edison General Electric Co. merged with the Thompson-Houston Co. to become the great General Electric Corporation, in which Edison was a major stockholder.

THE LESSON: THE POWER OF INCORPORATING

An innovation doesn't need to turn into GE to be considered successful. But incorporating gives legs to innovations. Will your innovation be changing lives in 10 years? 20? 50? If so, you need to recognize that you won't always be there. Creating a company as a support system for your innovation gives your innovation a future.

As the twentieth century began, Edison relentlessly invented more practical devices including the dictaphone, mimeograph, and storage battery. After creating what he called the "kinetiscope," he went on to introduce the film *The Great Train Robbery* in 1903, a breakthrough achievement that began to mix sound into the film industry.

World War I was on the horizon and the U.S. government requested that Edison assist in developing defensive devices for the ships and submarines of the navy. Throughout history, wartime has added an urgency to innovation. Either you adapt and evolve or you lose.

Edison passed away in 1931 with 1,093 patents in his name. His last patent was granted when he was 83 years old, a year before his death. There is no age limit for innovation.

Innovation is the result of an individual's sweat, effort, and perseverance. This is why we find an individual's name on each patent, as well as behind every great company created by an individual who has been inspired to question the way things are, rethink them, and do something about it despite the uphill struggle.

Chapter 3

PAIN

Walt Disney
Laugh-O-Gram Films

With every laugh, there must be a tear. This was the credo of the man whose name is now synonymous with imagination, Walt Disney. Motivated by the pain from his early failures and business decisions, Disney became one of the most financially successful dreamers in U.S. history.

You've heard of the conglomerate known as Disney. But its creator didn't strike gold the first time he started a company. Walt Disney's business ventures actually started with a small company in his hometown of Kansas City, Missouri, called Laugh-O-Gram Films. It's a good thing Disney saved his moniker for his second endeavor— "Laugh-O-Gram Land" just doesn't have the same ring to it.

With a contract in hand for six cartoon films, Disney founded Laugh-O-Gram in 1922 for just over $15,000 (approximately $200,000 in 2009 dollars [www.usinflationcalculator.com]). Despite creating early versions of such classics as *Cinderella, Alice in Wonderland* (then called the *Alice Comedies*), and *Little Red Riding Hood,* the company was soon wanting for revenue. The contracts—all from local movie theaters and businesses—simply didn't provide enough funds to keep the company afloat. By the end of 1922, Disney was suffering the humiliation of bathing weekly at the nearby Union Station because he couldn't afford to bathe at home.

Only a year after Laugh-O-Gram's doors opened for the first time, the company went bankrupt. Fortunately for every parent who has used a Disney film as a babysitter, Walt Disney was not out of dreams.

Instead of going back to work at a more stable job, he moved to Hollywood to start a new business. The failure of his first venture had inoculated him against letdowns. He would risk everything several times in his life to pursue his dreams. As a result, America and the world have treasures for the ages, made possible by a man who was not afraid to confront the prospect of pain.

He teamed with his older brother Roy in Hollywood. Together they pooled their modest resources and opened up the new Disney Studios in their uncle's garage. Disney resurrected the *Alice Comedies* and soon sold one of the featurettes to a New York firm owned by Margaret Winkler. The brothers took their profit and expanded to a real office in the back of another company.

What was different this time? Disney was making the same prints he had in Kansas City, albeit in a different place and with a different collaborator. Was it the magic of Hollywood? Perhaps that special Roy Disney touch?

In truth, it was neither. Rather, it was merely good timing made possible by a combination of communication and endurance.

While Disney was still running Laugh-O-Gram, he sent out dozens of letters to distributors claiming to have found "something new and clever in animated cartoons." No one took the bait. After all, Disney was completely unknown—why would a distributor take a risk on some small-town animator? Out of money, out of time, Laugh-O-Gram went under.

Disney sent out a second batch of letters in May 1923. This time, one of the letters reached the desk of the aforementioned Margaret

Winkler at exactly the right time. Winkler had been managing the accounts of two of the biggest cartoons of the time, *Felix the Cat* and *Out of the Inkwell*. At the time the letter arrived, the creators of those two cartoons were both threatening to leave and sign bigger contracts elsewhere.

Thus Winkler was more than happy to give Disney a chance. Under normal circumstances when other clients weren't rocking the boat, Winkler may not have even opened the letter. After all, at the time she was one of the leading distributors of animation in the world. But with her biggest two accounts halfway out the door, she had the time, resources, and need for something new.[1]

THE LESSON: THE POWER OF PATIENCE

Walt Disney was a persistent man who created from his pains and failures instead of wallowing in them. However, for an animator, he wasn't a patient man. He moved on projects without adequately anticipating the time and resources needed to realize them. Many times over his career he set himself up for failure or near-failure simply because he wasn't patient enough to plan ahead and give himself adequate time to succeed before diving into his next innovation.

If you open a restaurant in 2010, any restaurateur will advise you to obtain enough funding to keep the doors open for two years—ideally, three—even if your sales are woefully low. That time period gives you the chance to succeed. Few restaurants take off immediately. In the same way, few products are immediate hits with the public. There's a gestation period of acceptance during which sales are slow.

This isn't meant to discourage you from opening a restaurant or putting a new product on the market. Quite the contrary. Just give yourself time to succeed, and be patient enough to give your concept a chance.

Disney would learn a lesson regarding intellectual properties that would serve him for the rest of his career. The distributor for the *Alice Comedies* had convinced Disney that another character should be created to mimic and replace the production. Unbeknownst to

Disney, this would shift the intellectual property ownership from him to the distributor, a practice known as *work for hire*. Thinking the new creation was under his control, Disney created a new character called Oswald the Lucky Rabbit. When Disney was told that he was going to be replaced by the distributor's own animation team, he made a mental note not to make the same mistake in future negotiations.

■ ■ ■

The pain of losing his own creation inspired Disney to create his most endearing character, Mickey Mouse. He was also determined to create properties that he would exclusively own and control.

After changing the name of his creation from Mortimer to Mickey per his wife's advice, Disney handed his early sketches over to his close friend and chief animator, Ub Iwerks. Iwerks fine-tuned the art while Disney wrote the screenplay. The initial release was a silent film called *Plane Crazy*, but it failed to find a distributor.

THE LESSON: THE POWER OF A NAME

Would Mortimer Mouse have caught on as Mickey Mouse did? We may never know. We'll also never know if Laugh-O-Gram Films would have had the lasting appeal of Disney Studios. But it cannot be denied that there's power in a name.

When you create something new, you have the opportunity to select a name that might become the face of your brand for years to come. Ask yourself the following questions as you brainstorm:

- Does it make sense?
- Is it memorable?
- Is it easy to pronounce?
- Is the domain name available?

If you have a few names that sound good to you, run them by your friends to see what they like. It's only about $10 to reserve a domain name, so you could pick and register a few names if you're still undecided. If your mind is set on a ".com" name that has already been taken, you can bid on the name through services like snapnames .com. You can also add an extension to your company's name, such as Acmeco.com instead of Acme.com.

Following the failure to sell Mickey Mouse the first time around, Disney had a theory that something was missing. Sound was just being introduced into movies, allowing for extra dimensions to enhance the characters. Risking that most audiences weren't ready for the advancement, Disney provided a voice and personality for his marquee character. The squeaky voice of Mickey Mouse debuted in the cartoon film titled *Steamboat Willie* in 1928. It was an instant success.

■ ■ ■

Mickey Mouse became the flagship property of Disney and quickly surpassed Disney's erstwhile character Oswald. Disney's good fortune allowed him to continue to innovate; his next creation was a concept called *Silly Symphonies*. These musical shorts took full advantage of sound and animation. In addition, the *Silly Symphonies* received a boost from the invention of Technicolor, for which Disney obtained an exclusive agreement from Herbert Kalmus. Disney's first use of the new Technicolor in the musical short *Flowers and Trees* won an Academy Award in 1932. But the best was right around the corner. In the middle of the Great Depression, Disney created the best-selling cartoon short of all time, *Three Little Pigs*. The story of those little pigs struggling against all odds was exactly what audiences needed in the most difficult economic period in U.S. history.

In 1932, Disney received his first Academy Award for his creation of Mickey Mouse. In 1935, Mickey was brought to life in color for the first time, and supporting characters such as Donald Duck, Goofy, and Pluto soon followed. Disney possessed an insatiable appetite for innovation and he soon expanded his horizons to full-length animated movies.

Innovation often is preceded by skeptics. The news of Disney's attempt at an animated full-length feature of Snow White was dubbed by industry critics as "Disney's Folly." After all, cartoon shorts attracted a different audience—children with short attention spans—than the live-action, feature-length films of the day. In the 1930s, the average length for a live-action film was 96 minutes.[2] By contrast, *Steamboat Willie* was only 8 minutes long! Thus, the movie industry predicted not only that Disney's attempt would fail, but also that it would destroy the Disney Studio altogether. This pessimistic view was even held by his wife and brother, who tried to dissuade Disney of his plans.

Nonetheless, Disney pursued the project and spent every dollar he had to train his studio in the animation and film techniques that would be necessary to deliver his dream. He also employed Chouinard Art Institute professor Don Graham to develop an in-house training operation.

His critics were almost right. Disney ran out of money before the completion of *Snow White and the Seven Dwarfs* and had to present an unfinished cut of the movie to Bank of America to get a loan to finish the project. Disney's passion and demonstration of the rough cut were powerful enough to secure the money, and the film was completed in 1937. It premiered at the Carthay Circle Theatre on December 21, 1937, with a running time of 83 minutes.

The film received a wide release in February 1938 and was the first animated feature in Technicolor. It became the most popular film of 1938 and earned over $8 million in the box office. This triumphant innovation ushered in the golden age of animation. Soon to follow would be *Pinocchio, Fantasia, Bambi, Alice in Wonderland, Peter Pan,* and *Dumbo*.

Disney silenced his critics time after time by having the confidence to anticipate the future of entertainment. Putting users—the audience—first, he consistently adapted new technologies to improve their viewing experience.

MODERN PARALLEL: JOE JACOBSON, E INK CORPORATION

In 2009, the electronic-book market is exploding. E-book sales currently account for 10 percent of the overall market, up from less than 1 percent just two years ago. No one saw it coming. No one, that is, except Joe Jacobson, inventor of the e-ink technology that powers every major e-book on the market today.

Since the invention of the Guttenberg press in the 1400s, the method by which words are printed on paper hasn't changed much. The concept of *moveable* type—interchangeable individual letters molded from wood or cast iron—sustained the printing industry for hundreds of years. Modern adaptations have allowed for millions of copies of *Harry Potter* to be printed within a few weeks, but the basic concept hasn't changed much at all: words permanently stamped onto paper.

In 1993, Joe Jacobson, a researcher at the Massachusetts Institute of Technology (MIT), decided to figure out a different way. It was the beginning of the information age—computers and the monitors that displayed information were beginning to evolve. A single computer screen could display an infinite number of letter and word permutations. And yet the most familiar viewing surface of them all—a page of a book—was stagnant and still. Something had to change.

Jacobson was intrigued by the idea of pixels, the microscopic grains that comprise computer screens. A single pixel doesn't look like much, but put 300 of them together and you have a square inch of text. Why couldn't the same concept work for the book of the future, albeit without a backlight (to cut down on power requirements and eye aggravation)?

In 1996, he had his answer: e-ink. A single e-ink microcapsule contains tiny, two-tone particles. An electric field controls which direction the particles are facing. Suddenly he had a completely customizable, adjustable screen in his hands.

Jacobson helped to form the E Ink Corporation in 1997 with his invention as the foundation of the company. Immedia was the first company to use the technology en masse, followed by Sony with its Reader. The biggest boost to the future of the company came in 2007, when Amazon released its Kindle e-book to broad critical acclaim and an immediate backlog of orders. With updates to the Kindle and the Reader following over the next two years, along with a new batch of e-books from a variety of booksellers and manufactures, e-ink may be the most important innovation in publishing in hundreds of years.

Not only that, but with platforms like newspapers and magazines that depend on advertising revenue floundering in the poor economy, e-books provide cheaper distribution channels and immediate access to the people who are most likely to purchase new content. E Ink's explosion couldn't have happened at a more opportune time.

In the same way that Walt Disney pushed the envelope to bring new forms of entertainment to the masses, Joe Jacobson challenged the status quo and ushered in the first significant change in the printed word in more than 600 years.[3]

During World War II, the U.S. government took up most of the animation capacity of the Disney Studios, creating training and instructional films for the military. Disney also produced two morale-boosting shorts for the home front, namely *Der Fuehrer's Face* and *Victory through Air Power*, in 1943. During this period, Disney also started the tradition of re-releasing a feature film every seven years. *Snow White and the Seven Dwarfs* was re-released in 1944.

■ ■ ■

The post-war era of Disney was busy with more feature films and innovations. Most notably was the creation of *Cinderella*, which became the best-selling movie since *Snow White*. But the Disney innovation machine was active on all fronts, including a collection of cartoon shorts and full-length dramatic films that combined live action with animation, such as *Song of the South*. A new Disney category included live-action nature films titled *True Life Adventures*, and education films such as collaborations with NASA. However, this period was not without very stiff competition from the likes of Warner Bros. and its popular character Bugs Bunny.

While the competition was gaining ground, Disney was innovating for the future. His childhood was full of fond memories of trains, and this image never left him. He built a miniature railroad at his residence on Carolwood Drive in Los Angeles. This railroad theme would be carried through to his eventual theme park operations. As he watched his own children and friends enjoy the Carolwood Pacific Railroad, this became the inspiration to build an amusement park that his employees could enjoy. Central in his initial plans were two simple objectives: The park had to be like no other, and it had to be surrounded by a train. Thus, the seeds for Disneyland were sown.

THE LESSON: THE POWER OF BRANDING

If you're tinkering in your garage, you're probably not thinking about brand positioning and perception. It's probably too early for that. In Walt Disney's case, he spent years innovating the craft of animations and films, but it wasn't until he created Disneyland that he truly anchored the Disney brand.

Up until the point that Disneyland broke ground, audiences and Disney films were separate entities. People escaped into the films for an hour or so, but they didn't move from their seats.

Disneyland changed that. It was a place where you could go to actually be a part of the Disney fantasy universe—a place where trees sang and animals talked and pirates danced. By pulling fairy tales off the big screen and creating a real place in which to be a part of them, Disney Studios established itself as the company that makes dreams come true.

How do you want people to perceive your brand? If your company is Web-based, how can you position your brand in tangible reality so it makes a memorable, lasting impact on people?

During the 1950s, Disney expanded into full-length action features, including such classics as *Treasure Island*, *20,000 Leagues Under the Sea*, *Old Yeller*, *The Shaggy Dog*, *Pollyanna*, *Swiss Family Robinson*, and *The Absent-Minded Professor*. Disney Studios also saw a dual vision of TV production as it made films for the small screen, but also took the opportunity to provide the public an opportunity to watch the building of Disneyland. The TV presence of Disney evolved into the *Wonderful World of Disney*. In addition, during this period Disney developed its own music publishing company and licensing empire.

■ ■ ■

By the 1960, Disney had established itself as the world's leading pro-ducer of family entertainment. *Mary Poppins* was released in 1964 and was the blockbuster Disney movie of the decade, but Disney had once again expanded his innovation horizons. This time he envisioned an Experimental Prototype Community of Tomorrow, or EPCOT.

Unfortunately, he never got to see Disney World. Walt Disney had been a lifelong chain smoker and succumbed to lung cancer on December 15, 1966. The man whose business ventures started with a little-known company called Laugh-O-Grams left behind a legacy of moving pictures that will continue to entertain adults and children alike well into the future.

Chapter 4

INTUITION

Steve Jobs
Apple Inc.

Vision doesn't happen in a vacuum. Nobody knows this better than Steve Jobs and Apple Inc. Apple provides us with *the* example of the power of intuition.

Steve Jobs and Steve Wozniak became fast friends in 1972 at Hewlett-Packard where they were both employed. Jobs had just finished high school and Wozniak had just dropped out of college. Wozniak was an inventor; Jobs, an innovator.

In 1974, Wozniak invited Jobs to join the Homebrew Computer Club, an organization of computer enthusiasts. Jobs was working at Atari at the time. Wozniak pursued building computers as a hobby, but Jobs had a strong desire to commercialize computer technology. Jobs persuaded Wozniak to build a computer that they could sell to the public. In 1975, the two men worked from Jobs' house to collaborate on the first Apple computer. They used the Homebrew Computer Club as their board of advisers by presenting them with the progress they made every other week. In addition, they recruited another partner, Ron Wayne, a draftsman who worked with Jobs at Atari. He created the first Apple logo. His involvement was short-lived and they bought his 10 percent stake back for $800, as Wayne was fearful of the entrepreneurial environment. (Apple, Inc. is now valued at over $180 billion.)

THE LESSON: THE POWER OF EMPLOYEES WHO BELIEVE

Although Jobs may not have known it at the time, having Ron Wayne quit might have saved him a lot of needless time and energy. Wayne didn't believe that computers were worth the risk. He wasn't 100 percent behind the cause—maybe not even 10 percent.

Zappos, the Internet shoe retailer headed by CEO Tony Hsieh, employs a strategy to weed out workers who don't believe the Zappos mantra (which boils down to providing service that awes customers). Zappos doesn't wait until an employee has worked for the company for years—even months—before testing their loyalty. Instead, after a paid four-week training session, employees are given "The Offer":

> If you quit today, we will pay you for the amount of time you've worked, plus we will offer you a $1,000 bonus.

Some people—about 10 percent—take the money and run. The remaining 90 percent, the ones who believe in Zappos and want to work there, stay on. Zappos has some of the highest employee retention rates and positive ratings across the industry.

The investment you put into your employees is only worth as much as the investment of time, energy, and creativity that they put into your company.

The Apple I was a product that Jobs sold to the Byte Shop on spec in 1976. This enabled the two Steves to gain credit from the parts producers to purchase the necessary materials for the initial order. The Apple I was not a kit, but a self-contained unit. It was a simple machine, but it had some innovative features, including the ability to use a TV as a display screen. Most machines had no display capability at all. The user could also insert a cassette tape to save the programming. As promised, the Byte Shop received their order and Wozniak and Jobs were on their way to making Apple II, which would change the computing world.

■ ■ ■

By the following year, Wozniak had developed the Apple II and Jobs had sold the vision to an angel investor who funded the young start-up company. In addition, a new logo was designed. This simple trademark would become the banner of a computing revolution.

The Apple II, then the face of the home computer, was introduced first at the West Coast Computer Fair in April 1977. Millions of the Apple IIs were sold, establishing Apple as a major player in the emerging market. Wozniak remained the technology developer while Jobs took the position of vice chairman. The angel investor positioned a professional manager as president.

In 1979, Jobs arranged a tour of the Xerox PARC laboratories and saw the research being done on the graphical user interface (GUI) that allowed users to interact with Alto computing devices. During this visit he saw the future of home computers through the ease of use of GUI compared to the standard text-based interface. Jobs negotiated an agreement between the two companies to share research in return for pre-IPO shares.

THE LESSON: THE POWER OF NEGOTIATION

The key to effective negotiation is the strength to know what you're entitled to, the courage to walk away if you're offered something else, and the wisdom to know the difference.

A friend of mine is an excellent negotiator. His favorite story to tell involves a luxury car he had his eyes on. The car was listed at $40,000.

One day he went to the dealership, found a salesman, and said, "I'd like to buy that car."

The salesman's eyes lit up. Never had a sale been so easy! Before he started listing features and options, our friend held up his hand and said, "My offer is $28,000."

The salesman looked at him like he was crazy. "Sir," he said, "it's a $40,000 car. I can probably talk to the manager about knocking off $500 or so. . . ."

Our friend smiled and shook his head. "No, that's okay. Here's my number—give me a call when the price is $28,000."

And he walked away.

A few days later, he got a call from the salesman. "Sir, are you still interested in buying the car?"

Our friend assured him that he was. In response, the salesman offered him a discounted price of $38,000. The man politely turned him down, telling him to call back when the price reached his offer.

You see, all cars at dealerships have to be insured. So the dealerships lose money every day the cars sit on the lot. Not only that, but they're always in a race against time to sell the current year's cars before the next year's models are released. Thus the current year's cars lose value for every day that passes.

Did our friend end up getting the car for $12,000 off the sticker price? Not quite. He settled for a $10,000 discount. And he's been loyal to that dealership ever since.

The next six years were the first of the Apple revolution. In this period, the company introduced the Macintosh product line with its GUI-based system that would set the standard of computer interface forever. Steve Wozniak left the company, returned, and then made his final departure. The board brought in a former soft-drink executive to run the company, and Steve Jobs began to lose passion for the company he had founded. As the tumultuous 1985 came to a close, John Sculley, the new CEO, had removed Steve Jobs from the company, and sold the GUI system that Jobs had seen as the future of computing to Microsoft in exchange for the concession that Microsoft would continue to make its MS Word and Excel products for Apple computers.

■ ■ ■

In the meantime, Jobs was purchasing a visual effects house called Pixar. He also went on to found NeXT Inc., a computer company that built machines with futuristic designs and ran the UNIX-derived NeXTstep operating system. NeXTstep would eventually be developed into the Mac OS X. While not a commercial success due in part to its high price, the NeXT computer would introduce important concepts such as the severing as the initial platform for Tim Berners-Lee as he was developing the World Wide Web.

During the 12-year absence of Jobs at Apple, the company initially continued to grow on the backs of the two segmented systems of the Apple II and Macintosh lines. However, the company's growth began to slow as the IBM PC and its clones were rapidly selling. The competitive advantage that Apple had exclusively owned was lost, namely the GUI technology that had been licensed to Microsoft.

Apple's answer to the regression in sales was to use a soft-drink strategy of product segmentation, which did not serve the company well. The distribution system was not capable of supporting the strategy, and consumers and Apple enthusiasts were not pleased with the abandonment of its long-held philosophy of simplicity. In an attempt to compete with Microsoft, Apple made an alliance with IBM and Motorola to create a new computer platform that would use hardware from IBM and Motorola and software from Apple. This effort culminated in the creation of the Power Macintosh, which contributed to the spiraling downfall of the company. By 1996, the company was at its lowest stock price in 12 years and had devastating financial losses.

What did Jobs have that other Apple CEOs did not? Why would Apple end up succeeding under his leadership but not others?

Quite simply, terrible times call for good leadership—*great* leadership. Jobs had the intuition and foresight that other Apple CEOs did not.

He knew when to compromise and with whom to forge relationships and collaborations.

A similarly respected leader in a completely different field is Dr. James Andrews, a surgeon who can turn even the most terrible days for a professional athlete into the start of a very lucrative future.

MODERN PARALLEL: DR. JAMES ANDREWS, ANDREWS SPORTS MEDICINE AND ORTHOPAEDIC CENTER

If you're a sports fan—particularly baseball—you've seen this line on the sports page or on news tickers many times: "[Famous athlete] will visit Dr. James Andrews for reconstructive surgery." It's become such a commonplace line to read that you probably just brush over it and move on. Of course the athlete is visiting Dr. James Andrews. Who else would you go to?

Why is that? What makes Andrews so special?

The roots of Andrews' success lie with his grandfather, a farmer and self-taught country doctor. He urged Andrews to be a doctor through a traditional route of formal education.

Andrews played sports (football and track) through high school and college. He wrapped up his time at the university in three years, forgoing his final year of eligibility in order to start medical school early. His passion for and understanding of competition and athletes continued, so he decided to focus on sports medicine.

As Malcolm Gladwell discusses in his book *Outliers,* some of the greatest success stories are the result of hours and hours of practice. In fact, there's a specific amount of practice that seems to directly correlate to success: 10,000 hours. Thus, Dr. Andrews' decision to specialize in sports medicine early on and the ensuing job he got with sports doctor Jack Hughston helped him begin to accumulate those precious hours of practice early on. Now, after over three decades of experience in the niche market of reparative surgeries on athletes, Dr. Andrews has well exceeded those 10,000 hours. He's performed over 2,500 Tommy John surgeries alone (replacing a torn ligament in the elbow with a tendon; this surgery is generally used for pitchers whose elbows snap under the stress of throwing fastball after fastball).

It's not a coincidence that Gladwell also references Steve Jobs in *Outliers*. Ten thousand hours of intentional, focused practice makes a huge difference for success. For all you moonlighters out there, if you can spare four hours every evening, seven days a week, on this kind of focused practice, you should be an expert in your field in just under seven years.

Thanks to all that practice, Dr. Andrews honed his intuitive skills to the point that a casual conversation and checkup with an injured athlete can lead to an immediately, accurate prognosis. He processes a number of factors—physical, emotional, level of commitment, pain tolerance, and so on—to determine what needs to be done. When he enters surgery, he is completely calm and focused on the goal of repairing the injury. He's able to block out all external factors and pressure from coaches, agents, and family thanks to his years of experience.

But why do you and I know the name Dr. James Andrews? There are plenty of great doctors out there, many of whom treat celebrities.

The key is Andrews' ability to build and nurture a network of relationships. He founded a medical society with some other young doctors in the 1970s primarily for the purpose of networking (not just for referrals, but also for sharing successful techniques). He wrote chapters in textbooks and is a regular speaker at various conferences and events. Most important, of course, are the connections he's forged with high-profile athletes. He knows that if he does a great job for one athlete, the entire team is going to hear about it. Like Andrews, Steve Jobs would selectively forge strategic relationships with those from whom Apple would benefit.

Andrews' combination of experience, intuition, and relationships make him the premier sports surgeon in sports today. If your career is threatened by an injury, you know who to call.[1]

Steve Jobs returned to Apple in 1997 after he sold the NeXTstep operating system to his old company. Apple rehired him to guide the company in a new and profitable direction. Immediately, Jobs introduced the Apple online store, which was made possible by the WebObjects application server that had been developed by NeXT. The Apple store was part of the new made-to-order strategy first attempted by Dell in the 1980s.

■ ■ ■

Jobs saw a new future for Apple that included a new partnership with Microsoft. It culminated in a formal relationship he made with Bill Gates to develop more products for Apple and to be a new investor. Jobs stated the new relationship with Microsoft like this at the 1997 Macworld Expo:

> If we want to move forward and see Apple healthy and prospering again, we have to let go of a few things here. We have to let go of this notion that for Apple to win, Microsoft has to lose. We have to embrace a notion that for Apple to win, Apple has to do a really good job. And if others are going to help us that's great, because we need all the help we can get, and if we screw up and we don't do a good job, it's not somebody else's fault, it's our fault. So I think that is a very important perspective. If we want Microsoft Office on the Mac, we better treat the company that puts it out with a little bit of gratitude; we like their software. So, the era of setting this up as a competition between Apple and Microsoft is over as far as I'm concerned. This is about getting Apple healthy, this is about Apple being able to make incredibly great contributions to the industry and to get healthy and prosper again.

This incredible insight into a relationship that had more animosity than the New York Yankees and the Boston Red Sox was a dramatic shift in strategy for Apple.

To build the company and to introduce the new era of Apple, Jobs used lessons learned from his NeXT experience as Apple embraced futuristic designs for its new products. The iMac was introduced in

1998 and featured an integrated CRT display and CPU packaged in an innovative and compact translucent plastic body. Consumers readily accepted the product, buying over a million units. Mac was back and excitement grew to find out what Jobs had in store.

THE LESSON: THE POWER OF DESIGN

Aside from conceding a business relationship with Microsoft, the key for Apple's turnaround was rooted in attractive design. In the late 1990s, most computers looked exactly like one another. They all had the same gray, drab exterior and were somewhat complicated to set up.

Jobs turned the industry on its head by introducing the iMac. The bright, colorful design and translucent exterior assured consumers that computers could be fun—and easy to use. To set up an iMac, all you had to do was pull it out of the box and plug it in. The CPU and monitor were one and the same.

To this day, Jobs has continued to assert that Apple will put design and usability above all else. Instead of elaborate keyboards, iPods have wheels that are easy to manipulate with one hand. The iPhone utilizes intuitive gestures on its touch screen. And future iterations of the early iMacs—now called MacBooks—radiate prestige from their sleek, brushed aluminum exteriors.

The lesson is this: Don't underestimate the power of good design and intuitive user interface (UI). Whether you're inventing the car of the future (Toyota Prius) or programming the next big social networking web site (Facebook), the look and feel of the site may be the key to your success.

Although Jobs was forging new collaborations with Microsoft, he was pulling back licensing agreements that had been established for the Apple operating system with outside companies. Apple introduced more products, including the iBook, Power Mac 4, and the AirPort product series, which emphasized wireless LAN technology.

■ ■ ■

The second era of Jobs at Apple began in 2001 when he utilized the operating system from NeXT to create the Mac OS X. The new operating system combined the reliability and security of Unix with a completely overhauled and innovative user interface. This accomplishment led the way for a host of innovative products to be developed and a new distribution strategy to be introduced to the public.

Three dates in the year 2001 will go down in history as the three most important dates of the Apple Renaissance. On March 24, Apple introduced the Mac OS X version 10.0. This system would lead the way for some of the most successful product launches in consumer product history. Then on May 19, two Apple Stores opened (Microsoft didn't open its first brick-and-mortar store until October 2009). One of the stores was in Tysons Corner, Virginia, and the other in Glendale, California, at the Glendale Galleria. Last, on October 23, Apple introduced the iPod, a portable media player that revolutionized the portable music market. The iPod started as a five-gigabyte player capable of storing around 1,000 songs, which seemed like a lot at the time.

THE LESSON: THE POWER OF FACE TIME

Do its stores give Apple a competitive edge over other companies that exist solely online?

E-commerce is booming. Eighty-eight percent of all consumers have made purchases online, with Web-based sales forecasted to grow at a rate of 14 percent a year (compared to 2.6 percent for brick-and-mortar establishments). Companies like Amazon and ING avoid brick-and-mortar stores to save on costs, savings that they pass on to consumers (and use to attract new customers).

Apple could close all of its stores and probably continue to be successful. However, Steve Jobs understands the importance of face time, an underrated quality in the twenty-first century. Face time for Apple consists of two elements:

1. *Face time with the product.* As previously discussed, Apple products sell themselves with their design. Recall the first time you held

an iPod in your hand. The quality of the screen, the weight, the responsiveness of the scroll wheel—these are all elements that you couldn't have understood by looking at a photo or watching an introductory video online. If you have a product that people need to interact with to understand, you need to get it into a brick-and-mortar store.

2. *Face time with Apple geniuses.* Even the simplest computers are complex—and expensive—pieces of technology. For many consumers, having face time with an actual person (Apple calls its store employees its "geniuses") makes a huge difference when it comes to making a decision about a new purchase. In addition, when Jobs came onboard at Apple for the second time, he was fighting an uphill battle—Mac users consisted of only 5 percent of the overall market in 1998.[2] He needed a way to convince people who had been PC users for years that they could make the transition to Macs. Thus the mission of the Apple geniuses was born.[3]

The iTunes music store launched in 2003 with 2 million downloads in the first 16 days, all of which were purchased on Macintosh computers. It wasn't until later that Apple released a version of iTunes for Windows, allowing Windows users the ability to access the store. The iTunes software itself was free, openly available to anyone who owned a computer and had Internet access. In contrast, iPods were a few hundred dollars each (depending on capacity). It was through this price delineation that Apple positioned itself as a designer and manufacturer of hardware, not software.

■ ■ ■

Not only that, but Jobs positioned Apple as a *premium* vendor of computers (similar to the example of Velocity Micro in Chapter 2). Most Apple computers are priced at $1,000 or above. Because Apple focuses specifically on that lucrative market, as of June 2009, it controlled a whopping 91 percent of the market share for $1,000-plus computers.

THE LESSON: WHAT KIND OF COMPANY ARE YOU?

Quite simply, you can't do everything. Neither can your company. Instead of trying to do everything and ending up with 100 mediocre products, focus on the core elements that make your innovation special.

This applies particularly well to Web design. As cloud-computing software company 37Signals notes in its book *Getting Real,* the key to building a successful Web application is to build less:

> Conventional wisdom says that to beat your competitors you need to one-up them. If they have four features, you need five (or 15, or 25). If they're spending x, you need to spend xx. If they have 20, you need 30.
>
> So what to do then? The answer is less. Do less than your competitors to beat them. Solve the simple problems and leave the hairy, difficult, nasty problems to everyone else. Instead of one-upping, try one-downing. Instead of outdoing, try underdoing.

Whether you're executing a million-dollar idea for the first time or restructuring a company or product that's been around for a while, pick your battles. Decide what your company's all about and stick with it.

Two more groundbreaking innovations reconfigured Apple from a computer company to the diversified consumer electronics company called Apple Inc.

■ ■ ■

If there was any question remaining that Jobs and Gates saw each other as friendly competitors, the Apple introduction of the new Intel processor in 2006 would leave no doubt. This incredibly savvy strategic decision would in essence transform each Mac into two computers—one that could handle Apple software and one that could handle PC software.

The next Apple revelation happened after Apple and AT&T collaborated on the development of a new kind of phone. Inspired by Jobs' direction to investigate the use of touch-screen technology, the iPhone revolutionized the mobile phone industry. Like other Apple products, it took on a cult-like following that rapidly expanded beyond the bounds of Apple enthusiasts. The product was in such demand upon launch that consumers camped out in front of Apple stores to purchase one. Apple found itself a major player in the computer, music, and telecommunications industries. By November 2009, Apple had sold nearly 50 million iPhones.

Despite some health issues, Steve Jobs continues to embody the intuition he employed to resurrect Apple in 1997. One of Jobs's favorite quotes sums up his visionary style. "There's an old Wayne Gretzky quote that I love. 'I skate to where the puck is going to be, not where it has been.' And we've always tried to do that at Apple. Since the very, very beginning. And we always will."

Chapter 5

SIMPLICITY

Robert W. Johnson
Johnson & Johnson

S implifying problems is the essence of innovation. No company better exemplifies this power than Johnson & Johnson (J&J).

You don't remain one of America's most admired companies after over 123 years without finding simple solutions for complex problems. Johnson & Johnson is one of the largest health care firms in the world and one of the most diversified. Its operations are organized into three business segments: pharmaceutical, professional, and consumer.

Most of us know J&J by the simple solutions to everyday problems like skinned knees and headaches that it provides through its household products. They include Johnson's baby care, Neutrogena skin- and hair-care line, Tylenol and Motrin pain relievers, Stayfree feminine hygiene products, the Reach oral care line, Band-Aid brand adhesive bandages, Imodium A-D diarrhea treatment, Mylanta gastrointestinal products, and Pepcid AC acid controller.

The roots of J&J are found in a man named Robert Wood Johnson. As an apothecary in New York in the late 1800s, Johnson was inspired to solve a problem that had been discovered by Joseph Lister. Lister identified that airborne germs were the source of widespread infection in operating rooms. But Lister's solution for the problem was cumbersome and complex. He felt the best defense against airborne viruses was to spray each operating room with carbolic acid. Hospitals were eager to find a more workable solution that would protect patients from infection and, frequently, death.

Robert Wood Johnson solved the problem with a simple solution, and started his company, along with his two brothers, James and Edward, in an old wallpaper plant. The start-up venture began in 1886 and was incorporated in 1887 in New Brunswick, New Jersey. The actual product they made was a medicinal plaster composed of medical compounds mixed in an adhesive. It was an elaborate early version of the Band-Aid. Soon the Johnson brothers made even simpler versions of their initial product by creating a soft, absorbent cotton-and-gauze dressing, and Robert Wood Johnson's dream was realized. Mass production began and the dressings were shipped in large quantities throughout the United States. By 1890, J&J was using dry heat to sterilize the bandages.

This one simple observation and call to action, resulting in the development of modern-day bandages, would forever transform the health care industry. It also demonstrates that the best way to look for innovative solutions is to start by looking for problems. Sounds simple, but unfortunately it is an easy exercise that few people take the time to do. This early success also demonstrates Johnson's ability to link the logic of plaster and wallpaper. Today, this may appear an easy leap of logic, but in its day, the idea of taking an old wallpaper plant and revolutionizing the health industry was a very big stretch of the imagination.

Of course, the Johnsons didn't sit on their laurels, but immediately attempted to improve on every aspect of their simple solution system. The next undertaking was the establishment of a bacteriological laboratory in 1891. By the following year, the company had met accepted requirements for a sterile product. This was accomplished by introducing dry heat, steam, and pressure throughout the manufacturing process.

The Johnson brothers understood the need for effective communications and, in the second year of the company's existence, instituted a publishing arm of the company. This was much more than public relations—rather, this was educational training to their target market. Johnson & Johnson earned the trust of their customer base through helpful knowledge shared through publications. The brothers also had the foresight to recruit a qualified and professional writer to pen their many manuscripts. That man was Fred B. Kilmer, the father of the famous poet Joyce Kilmer. Fred was a well-known science and medicine writer. During his 45-year career at J&J, he wrote many useful articles, including *Red Cross Notes* and the *Red Cross Messenger*. The articles, which were widely read by physicians and pharmacists, encouraged antiseptic methods and recommended J&J products.

THE LESSON: THE POWER OF A COPYWRITER

"Tell me about your company."

People are going to say this to you if and when you start your own company. But what they're really saying is this:

"Tell me about your company *in 10 seconds.*"

Can you boil down your entire company, your innovation, your idea to a 10-second pitch? Once you exceed the 10-second mark in a pitch, you start to lose your audience. That's why screenwriters often present their ideas as mash-ups of other possible films: *Titanic* meets *The Fox and the Hound. Batman* meets *Love, Actually.* In just a few words, you paint a memorable picture for your potential investors and customers.

Writing good, clean copy is a skill that should not be underestimated. Take a look at the copy the next time you visit a new web site. Can you discern what the site or service is all about from the brief explanations on the home page?

TypeTribe went through this process when Jamey Stegmaier was selecting a tagline for the site. After many different iterations and focus groups, he settled on "Your Personal Critical Mass." The repetition of "-al" words isn't ideal, but otherwise the copy is clean and concise. Can you describe your innovation in four words?

In 1910, Robert Wood Johnson passed away. In some ways, a torch was truly passed to his brother James. Robert was the innovator, but James would be the builder, the one who would take the company from its simple roots to national acclaim. Although J&J had established itself as a solid company, James realized that both efficiency and expansion could be achieved simultaneously.

■ ■ ■

James began to vertically integrate the company to guarantee a source for the its increasing need for textile materials. Johnson & Johnson purchased Chicopee Manufacturing Corporation in 1916, and the first international affiliate was founded in Canada in 1919. A few years later, in 1923, Robert W. Johnson's sons, Robert Johnson and J. Seward Johnson, took an around-the-world tour that convinced them that J&J should expand overseas, and Johnson & Johnson Limited was established in Great Britain a year later. Diversification continued with the introduction in 1921 of Band-Aid brand adhesive bandages and Johnson's Baby Cream (Johnson's Baby Powder had debuted in 1893), as well as the debut of the company's first feminine hygiene product, Modess sanitary napkins, in 1927.

The younger Robert Johnson, who came to be known as "the General," joined the company as a mill hand while still in his teens. By the age of 25 he had become a vice president, and he was elected president in 1932. Described as dynamic and restless with a keen sense of duty, Johnson had attained the rank of brigadier general in World War II and served as vice chairman of the War Production Board.

THE LESSON: THE POWER OF LEARNING THE ROPES

There is much to be gained by starting from the bottom and working your way up, *even if you have the choice to start at the top.* You can learn so much from the foundations on which a company is built—the inner workings and politics of a factory floor, the ebb and flow of a retail store, the grind and grime of a construction site. When you inevitably reach the upper echelons of the company, you'll be the wiser.

Some companies take this into account when hiring new employees, especially for management positions. British Petroleum (BP) has a program for this—you're hired for a position in the BP corporate offices, but you start out working behind the counter in a gas station. You work your way up to manager of the gas station, and then you move on to a corporate position. By then you know from personal experience how a gas station works as an individual unit before you come to understand how it works as part of the organization as a whole.

Robert Johnson firmly believed in decentralization and was the driving force behind J&J's organizational structure, in which divisions and affiliates were given autonomy to direct their own operations. Simplicity of management is key to the building of a diversified company. It is impossible to require different kinds of divisions to operate under centralized and generic management policies. This simplified and decentralized system served J&J well as it diversified.

■ ■ ■

This strategy coincided with a move into pharmaceuticals, hygiene products, and textiles. During Robert Johnson's tenure, the division for the manufacture of surgical packs and gowns became Surgikos, Inc.; the department for sanitary napkin production was initially called the Modess division and then became the Personal Products Company.

Following his father's lead as a champion of social issues, Johnson spoke out in favor of raising the minimum wage, improving conditions in factories, and emphasizing business's responsibility to society. Johnson called for management to treat workers with respect and to create programs that would improve workers' skills and better prepare them for success in a modern industrial society. In 1943, Johnson wrote a credo outlining the company's four areas of social responsibility: first to its customers; second to its employees; third to the community and environment; and fourth to the stockholders. On the heels of the credo came the company's change from family-owned firm to public company, as J&J was listed on the New York Stock Exchange in 1944.

In 1959, J&J acquired McNeil Laboratories, Inc., maker of a non-aspirin (acetaminophen) pain reliever called Tylenol, which was at that time available only by prescription. Just one year after the acquisition, McNeil launched Tylenol as an over-the-counter (OTC) medication. Also in 1959, Cilag Chemie, a Swiss pharmaceutical firm, was purchased, followed in two years by the purchase of Janssen Pharmaceutica, maker of the major antipsychotic drug Haldol, which had been introduced in 1958.

Johnson retired in 1963. Although he remained active in the business, chairmanship of the company went outside the family for the first time. Johnson's immediate successor was Philip Hofmann, who, much like the General, had started as a shipping clerk and worked his way up the ladder. During Hofmann's 10-year term as chairman, J&J's domestic and overseas affiliates flourished. Hofmann was another firm believer in decentralization and encouraged the training of local experts to supervise operations in their respective countries. Foreign management was organized along product lines rather than geographically, with plant managers reporting to a person with expertise in the field.

Again, we see the advantage of keeping the rules simple and specific to the areas of expertise within the company. This decentralization and simplicity of focus plays an important role in the culture of J&J.

The early 1960s saw a stark increase in federal regulation of the health care industry. When James Burke—who had come to J&J from the marketing department of the Procter & Gamble Company—became president of J&J's Domestic Operating Company in 1966, the company was looking for ways to increase profits from its consumer products to offset possible slowdowns in the professional products divisions. By luring top marketing people from Procter & Gamble, Burke was able to put together several highly successful advertising campaigns. They first introduced Carefree and Stayfree sanitary napkins into a market that was dominated by the acknowledged feminine products leader, Kimberly-Clark. Usually limited to women's magazines, advertisements for feminine hygiene products were low-key and discreet. Under Burke's direction, J&J took a more open approach and advertised Carefree and Stayfree on television. By 1978, J&J had captured half of the market. Meantime, the company expanded its feminine hygiene line through the 1973 acquisition of the German firm Dr. Carl Hahn GmbH, maker of the o.b. brand of tampons.

THE LESSON: THE POWER OF CREATING A SOCIAL NORM

Burke engineered a marketing plan to make tampons less taboo, and in doing so, he secured a significant portion of the market for J&J.

Think back to 1999. Finding "matches," or dating partners, was a relatively new concept on the Web. People were starting to use the services to post profiles and find potential matches, but they didn't talk about it in public. The services didn't seem like legitimate ways to meet someone.

Then Match.com came along, followed by eHarmony. Both presented attractive, well-built sites with rapidly growing user bases. They advertised with campaigns like, "It's okay to look." Indeed, over time, it simply became okay to look—and okay to talk about. Today people talk about finding partners on those sites on the same level that they would talk about meeting someone at a bar or a party. It's simply another way to meet someone—it's no longer taboo.

How can you make your innovation a social norm?

One of Burke's biggest challenges was Tylenol. Ever since J&J had acquired McNeil Laboratories, maker of Tylenol, the drug had been marketed as a high-priced product. Burke saw other possibilities, and in 1975 he got the chance he was waiting for. Bristol-Myers Company introduced Datril and advertised that it had the same ingredients as Tylenol but was available at a significantly lower price. Burke convinced J&J executive management that they should meet this competition head-on by dropping Tylenol's price to meet Datril's. With chairman Richard Sellars's approval, Burke took Tylenol into the mass-marketing arena, slashed its price, and ended up beating not only Datril, but number one Anacin as well. This was a very simple strategy for a very complex organization.

■ ■ ■

Richard Sellars, Hofmann's protégé, had become chairman in 1973, and served in that position for three years. Burke succeeded Sellars in 1976 as CEO and chairman of the board, and David R. Clare was appointed president. Johnson & Johnson had always maintained a balance among the many divisions in its operations, particularly between mass consumer products and specialized professional products. No single J&J product accounted for as much as 5 percent of the company's total sales. With Burke at the helm, consumer products began to be promoted aggressively, and Tylenol pain reliever became J&J's number one seller.

At the same time, Burke did not turn his back on the company's position as a leader in professional health care products. In May 1977, Extracorporeal Medical Specialties, a manufacturer of kidney dialysis and intravenous treatment products, became part of the corporation. Three years later, J&J acquired Iolab Corporation, maker of ocular lenses for cataract surgery, and effectively entered the field of eye care and ophthalmic pharmaceuticals. In 1981, the company extended its involvement in eye care through the acquisition of Frontier Contact Lenses. The increased in-house development of critical care products resulted in the creation of Critikon, Inc., in 1979, and in 1983 Johnson & Johnson Hospital Services was created to develop and implement corporate marketing programs.

In September 1982, tragedy struck J&J when seven people died from ingesting Tylenol capsules that had been laced with cyanide. Advertising was canceled immediately, and J&J recalled all Tylenol products from store shelves. After the Food and Drug Administration (FDA) found that the tampering had been done at the retail level rather than during manufacturing, J&J was left with the problem of how to save its number one product and its reputation. In the week after the deaths, J&J's stock dropped 18 percent and its prime competitors' products, Datril and Anacin-3, were in such demand that supplies were back-ordered.

What did they do? They ran a simple advertising campaign. The company ran a one-time ad that explained how to exchange Tylenol capsules for tablets or refunds and worked closely with the press, responding directly to reporters' questions as a means of keeping the public up to date. The company also placed a coupon for $2.50 off any Tylenol product in newspapers across the country to reimburse consumers for Tylenol capsules they may have discarded during the tampering incident and offer an incentive to purchase Tylenol in other forms.

Within weeks of the poisoning incidents, the FDA issued guidelines for tamper-resistant packaging for the entire food and drug industry. To bolster public confidence in its product, J&J used three layers of protection, two more than recommended, when Tylenol was put back on store shelves. Within months of the cyanide poisoning, J&J was gaining back its share of the pain-reliever market, and soon regained more than 90 percent of its former customers. By 1989 Tylenol sales were $500 million annually, and in 1990 the line was expanded into the burgeoning cold-remedy market with several Tylenol Cold products; the following year saw the launch of Tylenol PM, a sleep aid. James Burke's savvy, yet honest, handling of the Tylenol tampering incident earned him a spot in the National Business Hall of Fame, an honor awarded in 1990.

THE LESSON: THE POWER OF MANAGING DISASTER

The true test for your company isn't finding funding or making a profit or going public. It's dealing with disaster.

When disaster strikes, how will you react, both in the short term and the long term? How will you manage the disaster in the face of the public? How will you respond to the uproar? How will you rebound?

Johnson & Johnson reacted to the Tylenol disaster by responding openly and transparently. They issued coupons to get people to try Tylenol again in order to regain their trust. And they added new layers of protection to the pills to keep the trust. They actually turned an incident that could have killed Tylenol into an opportunity to push Tylenol to the top of the market.

If you pay attention to Facebook, every few months there is an uproar over design change or privacy policy. Watch how Facebook responds. They usually respond almost immediately, but not in a reactionary way. They acknowledge that they hear people's concerns, and maybe they make some small immediate change to show that they actually care about what their users think. But in the end, they rarely— if ever—actually resort back to the status quo. Because in general, Facebook knows what it's doing. Design changes, for example, take months to plan and execute. They're very intentional changes meant to improve usability. Just because a few thousand people (out of the 350 million users on Facebook) express their distaste for the changes within a few hours of their implementation doesn't mean that Facebook should undo all those changes. But they should respond in a fast and transparent manner, turning a potential disaster into a way to build customer loyalty.

How will you respond when disaster strikes?

Burke and Clare retired in 1989 and were succeeded by three executives: CEO and Chairman Ralph S. Larsen, who came from the consumer sector; Vice Chairman Robert E. Campbell, who had headed the professional sector; and President Robert N. Wilson, who had headed the pharmaceutical sector. These three men were responsible for overseeing the network of 168 companies in 53 countries.

■ ■ ■

Larsen moved quickly to reduce some of the inefficiencies that a history of acquisitions had caused. In 1989, the infant products division was joined with the health and dental units to form a broader consumer products segment, eliminating approximately 300 jobs in the process. Over the next two years, the reorganization was extended to overseas units. The number of professional operating departments in Europe was reduced from 28 to 18 through consolidation under three primary companies: Ethicon, Johnson & Johnson Medical, and Johnson & Johnson Professional Products. In 1990, meantime, J&J formed Ortho Biotech Inc. to consolidate the company's research in the burgeoning biotechnology field, an area J&J had been active in since the 1970s.

Johnson & Johnson was able to counter increasing criticism about rising health care costs in the United States and around the world in the 1990s, in part because of the company's longstanding history of social responsibility. The company pioneered several progressive programs, including child care, family leave, and "corporate wellness," that were beginning to be recognized as health care cost reducers and productivity enhancers.

In addition, weighted average compound prices of J&J's health care products, including prescription and OTC drugs and hospital and professional products, grew more slowly than the U.S. consumer price index from 1980 through 1992. These practices supported the company's claim that it was part of the solution to the health care crisis. In 1992, J&J instituted its "Signature of Quality" program, which urged the corporation's operating companies to focus on three general goals: "Continuously improving customer satisfaction, cost efficiency, and the speed of bringing new products to market."[1]

Johnson & Johnson grew at a relatively slow pace in the early 1990s, in part because of the difficult economic climate. Revenues increased from $11.23 billion in 1990 to $14.14 billion in 1993, an increase of just 26 percent. A series of acquisitions in the mid-1990s, however, ushered in a period of more rapid growth, with revenues hitting $21.62 billion by 1996, a leap of 53 percent from the 1993 level. The skin care line had received a boost in 1993 through the purchase of RoC S.A. of France, a maker of hypoallergenic facial, hand, body, and other products under the RoC name. More significant was the acquisition the following year of Neutrogena Corporation for nearly

$1 billion. Neutrogena was well known for its line of dermatologist-recommended skin and hair care products.

Johnson & Johnson spent another billion dollars in 1995 for the clinical diagnostics unit of Eastman Kodak Company, which was particularly strong in the areas of clinical chemistry, which involves the analysis of simple compounds in the body, and immuno-diagnostics. In 1997, J&J combined its existing Ortho Diagnostics Systems unit with the operations acquired from Kodak to form Ortho-Clinical Diagnostics, Inc. (LifeScan, a J&J maker of blood glucose marketing kits since 1986, remained a separately run diagnostics company.)

Another subsidiary that grew through acquisitions in this period was Ethicon Endo-Surgery, Inc., which had been spun off from Ethicon in 1992 to concentrate on endoscopic, or minimally invasive, surgical instruments. Johnson & Johnson acquired Indigo Medical, which specialized in minimally invasive technology in urology and related areas, in 1996. Biopsys Medical, Inc., specializing in minimally invasive breast biopsies, was purchased in 1997. Another large acquisition occurred in 1996 when J&J spent about $1.8 billion for Cordis Corporation, a world leader in the treatment of cardiovascular diseases through its stents, balloons, and catheters. In 1997, in exchange for several consumer products, J&J acquired the OTC rights to the Motrin brand of ibuprofen pain relievers from Pharmacia & Upjohn. Other important developments during this period included the 1995 introduction of an Acuvue disposable contact lens, designed to be worn for just one day but priced at a reasonable level; and the 1995 U.S. approval of the antacid Pepcid AC, an OTC version of Merck's Pepcid that was developed by the Johnson & Johnson-Merck joint venture.

Today, Johnson & Johnson continues to be an innovation company based on a simple and decentralized management style that depends on people. Johnson & Johnson has more than 250 companies located in 57 countries around the world. The J&J family of companies is organized into several business segments comprising franchises and therapeutic categories.

MODERN PARALLELS: SIMPLE PROBLEMS, SIMPLE SOLUTIONS, SIMPLE PRODUCTS

This chapter wouldn't be complete without telling you about maybe the most used innovation that ever came out of J&J: duct tape.

But first, let's talk about a few modern innovations that have succeeded because they were designed with simplicity in mind from day one.

- *Pinkberry.* The frozen yogurt chain Pinkberry is one such innovation. In early 2004, Hyekyung Hwang opened a frozen yogurt store in West Hollywood where a tattoo parlor had once stood. Hwang saw the potential for a healthy, no-frills, delicious dessert, so she tested several recipes before creating two flavors (the only two flavors on the original Pinkberry menu): original and green tea. If you walked into that Pinkberry, you would realize right away that there's nothing else to buy—just one yogurt or the other. Not even water was available. By keeping it simple, there is little waste and a new staff member can be trained in a few hours. Pinkberry was making a profit by the end of the first month, was drawing between 1,300 and 1,600 customers a day by the second year, and had opened over 100 stores by the end of 2009.[2]

- *Flip Camcorder.* The Flip is a pocket camcorder made by a company called Pure Digital. It's a bare-bones device that does one thing well—and only one thing: it records digital video. Unlike most video cameras that require a manual to understand all the various buttons and settings and menu options, the Flip has three buttons: record, play, and trash. The replay screen is small, and the image looks much better on your computer than it does on the Flip. It's quite nearly foolproof, and because of the lack of bells and whistles, it takes only about two seconds to turn on. As another stroke of design genius, the recharger and the link to your computer are combined into a single USB drive that's built into the Flip itself. By early 2009, the Flip had commandeered a 13 percent market share in a competitive, overcrowded field.[3]

- *Nintendo Wii.* When Nintendo was designing its follow-up to the GameCube, it was faced with two next-generation products on the market from its major competitors: the Microsoft Xbox and the Sony Playstation 3. Microsoft and Sony had not only made machines that played complex, highly rendered games, but they also doubled as multimedia devices for playing music, connecting to the Internet, and watching DVDs and Blu-Ray discs (for later versions). So Nintendo had a choice: Try to replicate those companies' success, or do something different? They went all-in with the latter. Rather than making a machine that does everything, they created a less expensive device that simply played games. They marketed and designed it to appeal to the kid in all of us so that demographics other than hard-core gamers would be interested in the product. They created a device—the gyroscopic, motion-sensing remote—to make the games more intuitive so a new player wouldn't have to memorize 12 different button combinations. And they created games that didn't try to look photo realistic—they simply looked like *games,* colorful and playful and fun. This is not to say that the Xbox and the Playstation don't do well—they do—but Nintendo carved out a niche early on that created an entirely new type of demand in the gaming market.

Back to duct tape . . .

Johnson & Johnson had been making bandages, dressings, and other products for the military since the Spanish American War in 1898 and, during World War I, the company ran its surgical dressing production around the clock, seven days a week, to meet the needs of soldiers and hospitals. Doctors and surgeons needed *something* to keep the sterile dressings in place on the patient.

Given the company's long expertise in making adhesive tapes, the military asked Johnson & Johnson to have one of its operating companies make a waterproof, strong, cloth-based tape that could keep moisture out of ammunition cases.

The tape J&J designed was originally called "duck tape" for its water-repelling properties (duck feathers repel water). Soldiers soon discovered that the tape was incredibly useful in repairing just about anything that needed repair, from jeeps to planes to tents to boots. As time went on, "duck" morphed into "duct" because of its use in the postwar building industry to help connect ductwork for heating and air conditioning. The simplest of innovations sometimes provide the best—and most lasting—solutions.

Chapter 6

FAILURE

Milton S. Hershey
The Hershey Company

The sweetest success can come from the bitterest failures. This is the lesson of Milton S. Hershey and the Hershey Company, the largest chocolate manufacturer in America and a global icon that is recognized around the world.

Milton Snavely Hershey grew up in several small farming communities in central Pennsylvania and was influenced by a father who possessed an entrepreneurial spirit but did not have much success to show for it. Consequently, the Hershey family moved quite frequently as the elder Hershey tried new ventures that ranged from farming to producing cough drops. This transient existence and haphazard schooling did not serve Milton well. He was a poor student and eventually quit school after the fourth grade, which was not abnormal for that time.

THE LESSON: THE POWER OF QUITTING SCHOOL

You've heard the tales of current billionaires dropping out of college to pursue their true dreams. With the nuisance of formal education out of the way, people like Bill Gates, Steve Jobs, Michael Dell, and Kanye West went on to have extremely successful careers. American culture lauds these people for breaking the mold and pursuing their dreams.

The lesson here is not to actually quit school, especially not in fourth grade; rather, it's to take control of your education so it doesn't become something you want to quit. Take college classes that challenge you and stick with you, or sign up for courses that stretch your limits of discipline and teamwork. Use college as a social field on which you can sow seeds of innovation and networks.

As Hershey demonstrates, you may not need 18-plus years of formal education to be a successful innovator. But use his story to empower yourself to get the most out of your learning experience.

■ ■ ■

Hershey's father guided him toward learning a useful skill in a trade that he could master: He found him an apprenticeship with a local newspaper. Hershey did not care much for this profession and consequently did not perform his duties very well. He eventually got fired as a result of some serious mistakes he made while working the type-setting machine.

Hershey's mother still saw much potential in her young son and helped him find a profession and apprenticeship that would suit his talents and personality. He began his new apprenticeship at a confectioner in Lancaster, Pennsylvania. It was here that he would learn how to make candy and ice cream and begin to develop his own skills and nuances in the art of making confections.

Upon completing four years of training, young Hershey was inspired to move to Philadelphia to start his own candy business. His choice of location and timing were excellent, as Philadelphia was the site of the Great Centennial Exposition celebrating the 100th anniversary of the Declaration of Independence in 1876. He was suitably funded by money borrowed from his aunt and uncle. His list of products included taffy and caramels, all of which he made himself.

After six long and exhausting years of manufacturing candy at night, selling the confections during the day, and keeping the books in his spare time, Hershey collapsed under the strain of being a solo entrepreneur. The business went bankrupt.

THE LESSON: THE POWER OF ASKING FOR HELP

Many innovators will start out alone: the sleep-deprived inventor in the basement; the solitary employee who stands up to decades-old business practices; the solo musician who strings together chords that have never met before; the writer who toils away into the night while the world sleeps.

These are the stories that inspire us to change the world. If that person could do it by himself, why can't I? As the Introduction of this book notes, innovation is indeed a solitary activity.

However—and this is a very important "however"—if you are unable to ask for help when you truly need help, you will fail. Hershey learned this lesson the hard way, and by way of failure, he learned that he needed help. He needed someone to take the burden of time off his back so that he could actually sleep or get a few minutes of much-needed relaxation.

You can't do it all yourself. At some point you're going to need to get a secretary or a drummer or an editor. When that time comes, will you be able to put ego and ambition aside to ask for help?

■ ■ ■

Hershey may have been discouraged, but you wouldn't know it as he started to plan his next business move. He pulled up stakes and moved to Denver, where his father had moved after separating from his mother. It was here that he became an employee again at a candy manufacturer. However, this employment opportunity allowed him to learn a new method of making caramels using fresh milk. The technique made the caramels naturally chewy (many manufacturers added paraffin to create chewiness) and dramatically increased the product shelf life. This new skill would inspire him to launch a new entrepreneurial venture.

Hershey and his father moved around—to Denver, New Orleans, and Chicago—to check out business opportunities.

In 1883, Hershey moved to New York and thought if he could make it there, he could make it anywhere. His plan this time was to work for someone full-time and make his own confections independently on the side. He found employment at a candy company called Huyler and Company, and in his spare time created Hershey's Fine Candies. This moonlighting strategy had its advantages as it provided the irrepressible entrepreneur with a steady income while he developed his small company.

Unfortunately, Hershey experienced his first battle with changing commodity prices. Sugar prices skyrocketed that year and wiped out his working capital. Under the burden of multiple leases, he lost his candy-making equipment and was forced out of business. This failure brought some additional bad news as his family was fed up with his bright ideas and refused to loan him any more money. Consequently, he returned home to Lancaster, down but certainly not out.

THE LESSON: THE POWER OF REJECTION

Say you come up with the perfect twist on an existing Web service. You plan it, you raise the funds for an experienced developer, you market it with some clever promotions. And then . . . nothing. Nobody uses it. Your traffic is nonexistent. Your ingenuity has been rejected on a mass scale.

At that point, you have two choices: You can blame the customer or you can blame yourself. You can conclude that the customer is too stupid to know how great your web site is. The customer doesn't realize what they're missing. Your service is too good, too perfect—if the customer doesn't realize that, you don't want their business anyway.

Or you can learn from the rejection and constructively blame yourself. Maybe you just created a service that people don't need.

Maybe the design isn't very user-friendly. Maybe you should have made an iPhone app instead of a Web application. Maybe the concept is too hard to understand, and you need to simplify it.

The key is to listen and learn from those who reject your ideas. Yes-men are handy for everyday encouragement, but in the long run, the people who will give your innovation legs are those who reject you.

■ ■ ■

Upon returning to his hometown, Hershey set out to redeem himself and to fulfill his vision of making and selling candy. This time he took a different approach. He did not solicit his family, but instead convinced his Aunt Mattie to take a loan against her home to help finance yet another Hershey endeavor into the entrepreneurial world.

Hershey and his old employee William Henry Lebkicher begged, borrowed, and begged some more to scrounge up enough money to start the new Lancaster Caramel Company. The company introduced a new innovative product made from fresh milk, named the Hershey Crystal A caramels. These delicious treats caught the attention of an English importer who ordered £500 worth to ship back to the United Kingdom. This single order provided the necessary working capital for the young company to purchase additional equipment to expand. It also provided the necessary collateral to get a loan from the Lancaster National Bank.

After repeated failed attempts and the embarrassment of disappointing family and friends who had helped him financially on his journey, Hershey, Lebkicher, and oft-overlooked business manager William Blair had found a recipe for success.

THE LESSON: THE POWER OF A SINGLE CUSTOMER

Pi Pizzeria in Nantucket, Massachusetts, had its big breakthrough when President Obama declared it his favorite deep-dish pizza. Obama bought only a few pizzas when he stopped by the restaurant on the campaign trial in 2008, but he ended up helping Pi sell thousands more pizzas than they would have otherwise.

The power of a single customer should not be underestimated. Many businesses survive off of contracts with a single customer, often the government. That's a risky practice, because if you lose that one customer, you lose the business. More important is the mind-set that you just need to get that one customer—sometimes it's your first customer—in order to have a big breakthrough. Don't try to market to every possible customer. Instead, focus on a few key customers that can make a difference in your company's future.

In his book *The Tipping Point,* Malcolm Gladwell talks about "connectors," people who seem to know everyone. We all have a few friends who are connectors, and maybe you're one yourself. Technology has made it easier to find the connectors of the digital realm. If you're using Twitter to market a new product, you could blast an update to your 2,000 followers, a few of whom might pay attention; or you can use programs like Tweetake and IceRocket to isolate a few followers who have multitudes of followers themselves and direct-message them. Or look on Facebook for people who have a lot of Facebook friends and get multiple responses on their status updates. Or use Google Reader to find people with well-read blogs and contact them for their endorsement.

You can't reach everybody, especially not in the beginning when you're trying to get the word out about your innovation. But sometimes you can cause a bigger ripple in the pond by reaching that one key customer that will take your company to the next level.

■ ■ ■

From that success, Hershey was off to the races. The Lancaster Caramel Company continued to introduce innovative products and develop candy-manufacturing facilities across the country. New products included The Jim Cracks, Roly Polies, Melbas, Empires, Icelets, and Coconut Ices. To manufacture and distribute these candies, plants were built in Mount Joy and Reading, Pennsylvania; and in Chicago and Geneva, Illinois. By 1893, the Lancaster Caramel Company was employing 1,400 people.

Hershey's vision of a candy factory was finally beginning to take shape. To complete some research on European methods of chocolate making for the purpose of flavoring his best-selling caramels, he visited the Columbian Exposition in Chicago, which celebrated the 400th anniversary of the arrival of Christopher Columbus in America. More importantly, he was able to speak with equipment suppliers who provided the necessary chocolate-rolling machinery for building a factory in America.

At the time, most milk chocolates were made by hand in Europe and were very expensive to produce because of the labor intensity of the process. Hershey was convinced that he could mass-produce milk chocolate, making it affordable to the masses. He was so convinced of this that he ordered a chocolate-rolling machine from the German firm J.M. Lehmann Company.

THE LESSON: THE POWER OF SCALABILITY

We only know about Hershey in 2010 because he made the choice to mass-produce his milk chocolates. There are thousands of small chocolatiers in towns and cities across America, some of which do good business, but most people will never hear of them because their scale is very limited. When you only make 75,000 candies a year, there's a limited number of people who can consume them.

Purchasing the equipment and scaling up to mass-produce chocolate was a huge risk for Hershey. What if it didn't work? He would be left with a machine that could make a million chocolates a year and only a few mouths that wanted them. But he went big, diversified his product line, and reached people at a time when they were used to spending more for the same amount of chocolate.

Hershey paid close attention to sales and responded to meet demand. He structured the entire company around the idea that he could make huge amounts of chocolate very quickly at low prices.

He chose the level of supply he wanted to meet instead of waiting for market to dictate demand.

The idea is to take control of your target market by building your company on the ideal scale for your innovation. You want to meet a small, local demand? Then go small. You want millions of customers around the globe? Then structure your entire organization around going big.

■ ■ ■

In 1894, Hershey established the Hershey Chocolate Company as a subsidiary of the Lancaster Caramel Company. His first lines of production focused on a limited number of items, including baking chocolate, breakfast cocoa, and sweet chocolate coatings that were used in caramel production. Hershey spent a great deal of time and energy perfecting his recipe for milk chocolate. When he finalized the perfect recipe, he began to introduce a number of new chocolate items, including novelties such as chocolate cigars. He introduced over 100 new chocolates, but more importantly decided to concentrate his focus and financial resources on the making of chocolate instead of other candies.

This led him to some major strategic decisions that would change the course of the company and build one of America's most admired brands of all time. In 1900, he decided to sell the Lancaster Caramel Company to his competitor for $1 million and devote all his efforts to building the Hershey Chocolate Company. He retained the right to sell his competitor the chocolate that it would need in the future. The same man who had dropped out in the fourth grade had the business savvy of an educated business veteran.

Hershey had been planning this transition for some time. He had previously purchased his homestead in Hackersville in 1897 and now purchased 1,200 acres of surrounding land in nearby Dauphin County to build his chocolate factory. In addition, he had the vision to conceive of an ideal living community around the factory for the many workers he would need.

MODERN PARALLEL: BRIAN WELLINGHOFF, BARRY-WEHMILLER

In a time when working conditions in America were far beneath modern standards, Milton Hershey took a novel approach to human resources: He built his company around meeting employees' needs and keeping them happy. It sounds a bit like Google, but 100 years earlier.

You've heard many company executives say that humans are their most important resource. But how many really mean that? How many structure every aspect of their business around empowering individuals to get meaning and satisfaction from their work?

In 2002, the CEO of Barry-Wehmiller, Bob Chapman, sat down with Directors of Motivation Rhonda Spencer and Brian Wellinghoff. Barry-Wehmiller, a supplier of engineering consulting and manufacturing technology solutions, was facing a new era of manufacturing in which competitors' American factories were being shut down and the work outsourced overseas. The company had made a lasting commitment to be a great American company serving global markets, and Chapman, Spencer, and Wellinghoff wanted to find a way to keep that commitment—and their competitive edge—by maximizing the talents of their most valuable resource: their employees.

The company had recently acquired a large manufacturing facility in Green Bay, Wisconsin. The owner of that facility was vocal about the *lean manufacturing* process he had incorporated into the company's structure, and he was urging Chapman, Spencer, and Wellinghoff to give it a try in other factories owned by Barry-Wehmiller.

The three of them recognized the strengths of lean manufacturing. Lean's reputation was that it could help to improve the manufacturing process by making it more efficient and less wasteful, thereby improving the overall profit margins for the company. Lean's focus was to look at a facility's established processes from a technical standpoint and cut out the fat. The bottom line was to figure out what was best for the company as a whole.

The problem that Chapman, Spencer, and Wellinghoff recognized was that employees who were far removed from the benefits of a company's growing profit margins didn't necessarily care about making their work more efficient. The benefits weren't communicated to them, and they certainly didn't make a difference in their paycheck. They had always felt like cogs in the machine, and lean merely solidified that role.

Something clicked when the topic came up about how employees felt. Why not take their feelings into account? As efficient as Ford's assembly lines of old were, employees weren't—and never would be—emotionless automatons. They were people with the potential to do great, satisfying work—if given the chance.

Wellinghoff recognized an opportunity to make an innovative change across the spectrum of Barry-Wehmiller, which at the time owned a number of facilities across America, the United Kingdom, Italy, Hungary, and Belgium. As the meeting came to a close, he offered to spearhead an initiative to create a new form of lean manufacturing that would change the face—and the internal structure—of Barry-Wehmiller for the better.

Thus he created L3, the Living Legacy of Leadership.

There's a good chance that Barry-Wehmiller makes the machine that assembled the box containing the cereal you ate for breakfast this morning. To have the capability of cutting, printing, folding, and gluing that box, the machine requires hundreds of components that arrive at different times, are stored and constructed in multiple areas, and handled by many different people working different shifts at the manufacturing facility. Creating a single machine is an extremely complicated process, and for a single employee, it's tough to see how your contribution plays into the final result.

Instead of focusing on what's good for the company as a whole when it comes to making that machine, L3's focus is on the employees themselves: What makes their jobs more fulfilling? Sitting around waiting for a part to arrive isn't fulfilling. Nor is completing a redundant task that's been a part of the standard procedure for years. The challenge is recognizing those unfulfilling elements, communicating them, and then making a change happen.

Wellinghoff realized that the key to L3 was empowering employees to make small improvements for themselves, thus benefiting the company as a whole. So he structured L3 around two components: vision and inspiration.

Every new L3 process starts with a visioning process. Instead of calling a meeting of the company's executives, an L3 visioning session comprises a cross-functional group of people from all different levels and responsibilities. As Wellinghoff puts it, "Everyone is entitled to an inspiring vision of how their contribution makes a difference."

This cross-functional group engages in a dialogue intended to stretch their minds by pushing them into a deep conversation about their jobs. This isn't a first-date kind of conversation—this is a heavy discussion about the way the manufacturing facilities function.

From that original visioning session stems a number of smaller, ongoing dialogues—in essence, when L3 starts, it never stops. Many Barry-Wehmiller facilities utilize daily touch meetings that aren't necessarily as deep as the original visioning session, but they serve to keep communication open 24/7. Employees meet for a few minutes every morning to have an open chat about their jobs and their lives. It's a chance for them to build a connection with one another. As a result, they're more apt to share information during regular work hours that can make their jobs easier and more efficient—and, most importantly, more fulfilling.

You might think that employees would resist the idea of sharing their personal lives in an open meeting every day. You might also think that team leaders would see such meetings as a waste of valuable work time. But Wellinghoff, an analytical, by-the-numbers person himself, realized that there's a huge amount of value added when people are able to communicate outside of facts and logic. Whereas lean is purely results-driven, L3 asks employees, "How does this make you feel?" Once you get to that level, you're able to truly address employee satisfaction. Sure, Joe Worker makes 130 widgets a day on average. But is he fulfilled? If the company is 100 percent in support of his fulfillment, Joe is going to make the best widgets he possibly can.

The key to the type of results that L3 looks for is the second element, inspiration, which consists of hands, heads, and hearts. Wellinghoff uses the example of the *Wizard of Oz* when describing the difference between L3's concept of inspiration and the old way of thinking. The old way has employees recognizing the potential for positive change, but they don't feel empowered to do anything about it. "If only we had senior leadership support," they think.

L3's inspirational approach seeks to empower the employees to look to themselves to make a difference. It asks employees to do what they can with the tools they have, their growing sphere of influence from the visioning process and daily touch meetings, and the abilities they have to make the change spread across the facility. This is certainly slower than an executive mandating that a specific change be made immediately, but it has much longer-term results. Plus, because the change is led by employees at the ground level—people who have firsthand, daily experience on the factory floor—it's more likely to have a positive impact.

Has L3 made a difference at Barry-Wehmiller? The results speak for themselves. Since implementing L3 in 2003, Barry-Wehmiller hasn't sent a single American job overseas. Its Baltimore facility, one of the first to incorporate L3, doubled its inventory turn rate within just five years. And the company's marquee facility in Green Bay, plagued in 2003 by poor on-time performance and a senior leadership team that was completely out of touch with the ground level, has experienced a $52 million turnaround.

Barry-Wehmiller is so confident in the success of the L3 program that it now teaches the concept at its leadership university. The best administrators in the company are professors at the university. By establishing a program to teach L3 to new acquisitions, Barry-Wehmiller has created a living legacy of leadership that will allow it to keep its commitment to be a great American company serving global markets for years to come.

■ ■ ■

Hershey built the plant and the town to make a single product, the Hershey's Milk Chocolate Bar. Later, his chemists would figure out a recipe for a chocolate bar that could be mass-produced and sold for pennies. The consumer acceptance was immediate and the demand was end-less. The desire for this new product was so strong that Hershey's did no mass media advertising until 1970. Hershey had a keen eye for innovative self-promotion and purchased a Riker electric car in 1900, painted it with a Hershey's Cocoa logo, and had salesmen use it for deliveries in and around Lancaster. It cost $2,000 to produce and ran on batteries. This promotional vehicle drew almost as much attention as the candy bar itself. Hershey had a well-established and successful national sales and distribution team through the Lancaster Caramel Company.

THE LESSON: THE FALLACY OF "IT'LL SELL ITSELF"

Hershey created a delicious product at an affordable price. He could have then sat back, content that his creation was good enough to sell itself.

Go to your door and look outside. Are people lined up to buy your innovation? Probably not (at this hour, hopefully not!). Customers simply aren't going to go to you to buy your product, no matter how amazing it is.

There are a million ways to market a product; I won't go into them here. The point is to put your ego aside and realize that you need to spend the time and effort to let people know that your brilliant innovation exists. Those who wait to be discovered are setting themselves up for disappointment.

■ ■ ■

To say that the company and the town prospered would be an understatement. The Hershey Company and community grew at an exponentially rapid pace. Within 20 years the company had sales of approximately $20 million and the community had a school, hospital, and even a zoo (the cages weren't made of chocolate).

In 1929, the stock market crashed and the resulting depression gripped America, wreaking havoc on cities across the country. The Hershey Chocolate Corporation and the town of Hershey did not suffer the same kind of experience. Hershey not only protected current employees from the depression, but actually added 600 additional employees to the payroll during those tough times (most of the new employees were added to Hershey's sister business, Hershey Estates, in construction jobs related to new business work).

How did Hershey grow the company when so many other companies were failing? The key was that he had made sure that the company had cash reserves available for when the economy went downhill (not to mention the viability of a cheap, delicious product). While banks around the company were failing and people were begging for work, Hershey created new opportunities with the extra cash the company had accumulated over time.

To put that cash to use, Hershey began a building project in 1929 that put many people to work and lasted until 1939. They built a hotel, high school, community building, sports arena, and new air-conditioned headquarters building. Hotel Hershey reflected many of all the favorite things that Hershey had experienced on his trips throughout the world. The Great Depression was a time of great innovation and expansion for the Hershey Chocolate Corporation. New products such as the Krackle Bar, Mr. Goodbar, Hershey's Miniatures, and of course Hershey's Kisses milk chocolates were sold all over the world. Hershey never forgot the lesson he had learned in his failed operation in New York when the price of sugar skyrocketed. In preparation for the next price hike, he had purchased land and mills in Cuba. This time, as sugar prices went through the roof, he was ready.

As America moved from the Great Depression into World War II, Hershey continued to create innovative products that could be used by the United States military. As part of a soldier emergency survival kit, Hershey's developed Field Ration D bars that were four ounces and packed with extra calories and vitamins. Hershey produced over a billion of these bars during wartime. Accordingly, Hershey was presented the Army-Navy "E" award five times for civilian contribution to the war effort.

THE LESSON: THE POWER OF R&D

Research and development is an oft-overlooked area of established companies. If they have tried-and-true products and a marketing team to slap "New and Improved" on those products at key times, why would they need to spend money on risky innovations?

The truth is that R&D is at the heart of innovative success, particularly in terrible times. Hershey exhibited this understanding during wartime just as Disney did with flight training films. While the rest of the company is focused on being successful *today*, R&D can look 5 or 10 years down the road to see what's next. Or they can whip something clever together when the unexpected happens.

At the beginning of your innovation, *you* are R&D. But if your idea takes off and you form a company around it, make sure to invest the necessary funds and resources in R&D. It just might be your saving grace when times get tough.

■ ■ ■

Hershey was an innovator who never forgot his roots nor his struggles as a young boy. In 1909, Hershey and his wife established the Hershey Industrial School (today it is the Milton Hershey School) to help orphaned boys learn a trade in farming or industrial work so they would become able to support themselves. After his wife died in 1915, Hershey transferred his ownership of the Hershey Chocolate Company (then valued at $60 million) to the school trust fund in her honor. Today the school is sustained through its trust, which owns 40 percent of the stock of Hershey Foods and controls 75 percent of the voting shares.

The town of Hershey, Pennsylvania, is still home to about 9,000 people and draws over 40 million visitors each year. The company, school, and town are all testaments to the power of failure.

Chapter 7

FAITH

Mary Kay Ash
Mary Kay Cosmetics

Faith is an intangible quality that allows people to persevere when times get tough. It provides the supernatural strength to carry on when everything seems lost.

Mary Kay Ash had faith. This one guidepost was instilled in every policy and program that she developed over the years. She would build a company that allowed women to advance by helping others to succeed. Mary Kay Cosmetics' slogan was, "God first, family second, career third." This credo expressed Ash's desire for her associates to keep a balanced, ordered life, with faith at the top of the list.

Like most innovators, she had figured out a better way to do something and was determined to accomplish this no matter the odds.

Ash founded Mary Kay Cosmetics in 1963, after 25 years of direct selling for other companies. Her sales experience gave her the knowledge and direction she needed to found the company that made her famous.

Ash started out as a sales representative for Stanley Home Products, making appointments at people's homes. She recruited other women as salespeople because Stanley paid a small commission for the sales of each person she recruited. She eventually signed on 150 women and received a percentage of the sales from each one.

She had gained sufficient knowledge of the benefits of having commissioned sales reps, but knew that there was a better way to treat people based on the Golden Rule.

The end of her corporate career began in 1959, when Stanley asked her to move to another city and forfeit the small commission that she generated from establishing the 150 salespeople she had recruited. Soon afterward, she became a representative for World Gift Company, where she quickly became its national training director. However, she had experienced enough of the direct selling industry to determine that she had a better idea. She resigned from World Gift in 1963.

Interestingly, she started a company with a philosophy, but without a product. She was so convinced that her better way of structuring employees would simply need quality products to fill the pipeline. This reverse order of starting an enterprise was a testament to her vision of a superior way to treat people.

THE LESSON: INNOVATION IS ABOUT MORE THAN JUST A PRODUCT

Just like Mary Kay Ash, you don't need a product to start a successful, innovative company. Everyone's an inventor. Whether you create a brilliant device or you "invent" a new sandwich at lunch today, you're probably an inventor a thousand times over. But only a few people have the power to be successful innovators. Those people are the ones who don't just innovate a product (or a sandwich)—they're the ones who innovate customer service, human resources, marketing, and all the other areas that a business comprises.

Take, for example, Zingerman's Deli in Ann Arbor, Michigan. Zingerman's places a fair amount of importance on the quality of its food, but what it's famous for is its innovative approach to customer service. It isn't just about cashiers smiling at customers—it's an entire business model built around providing spectacular service and recognizing employees who go out of their way to provide it.

What innovative approach will set you apart from the rest?

Ash decided to start a direct sales company. After deciding on a structure, she chose a line of skin care products she had been using for more than a decade as the featured product. She had been introduced to the skin care products while she was selling Stanley products at a home party. The hostess, a cosmetologist, was testing these products on her friends. This woman had developed the products from a leather tanning solution her father had formulated, after he noticed how young his hands looked from using the solution every day. Ash bought the formula from the family. Ash lived by the Golden Rule, that she would treat people the way she would like to be treated. She probably could have stolen a sample of the tanning solution and rebranded it as her own. But instead she did the right thing and bought the rights to it. A sense of fairness was instilled in her every action.

■ ■ ■

Ash and her husband invested their life savings of $5,000 to rent a small office and manufacture an initial inventory of skin care products. They also recruited nine independent sales representatives. This kind of commitment is not unusual to great innovators because they truly believe that what they are doing is not only the right thing to do for themselves, but more importantly the right thing to do for others.

Only a month before the company was to open for business, Ash's husband died. Ash was devastated, but she decided to proceed with the opening anyway to honor the hard work he had put into forming the company. Her 20-year-old son, Richard, quit his job and ran the financial and administrative operations. Within the year, Mary Kay's other son, Ben, moved his family to Dallas and went to work for the family company as well. Daughter Marylyn joined the company later, becoming the first Mary Kay director in Houston.

THE LESSON: THE POWER OF SHARING YOUR PASSION . . . WITH EVERYONE

So you've come up with a great idea and a brilliant way to execute it, but you need funding to make it happen. Who do you turn to?

The obvious answer is family and friends, but it's tough for most people to ask those people for money. Ideally we'd all have anonymous groups of angel investors who believe in every idea we think of. But that's simply not the case. The people who already believe in you are your friends and family.

That's not to say that you can just send an e-mail to everyone in your address book and expect for them to fork over thousands of dollars. You need to present a compelling argument for someone who cares about you to share in your passion. Remember that you're presenting them an opportunity—you're not asking them to make a sacrifice or strictly to do you a favor.

Take the time to compose a letter that explains your idea, how you plan to execute it, and why your friends and family should share in that passion. Don't make it so short that people think you haven't thought through the idea, and don't make it so long that people discard it before finishing your letter. One page is ideal. If you have other details you'd like to cover, include a separate FAQ page with short questions and answers.

You can't depend on friends and family to make your company a success. But it's worth asking them to share in your passion and give you some funding to get your company off the ground. They deserve that, and so do you.

One of the small but important features of Mary Kay Ash's business philosophy was that she not only respected her commissioned reps, but in turn required them to respect the business by making a small investment into it. This may sound minor, but she clearly understood the advantage of having people committed with their own money, even if the amount was very small. Doing so reminded her people that it would take an investment of money, time, and effort for them to be successful.

Beauty by Mary Kay opened on Friday, September 13, 1963. The products were manufactured by a Dallas company and sold through a network of salespeople who were called "beauty consultants" and were required to purchase an initial "Beauty Showcase" kit. The beauty consultants were trained in scheduling and conducting Mary Kay parties, or "skin care classes," in private homes. Beauty consultants purchased Mary Kay products at 50 percent below retail and resold them with a markup. They also received commissions for sales made by salespeople they recruited. Ash had seen the long-term effectiveness of that structure at Stanley Home.

The company differentiated itself in several ways from companies that used illegal pyramid schemes. Mary Kay sold its products to all of its consultants for the same 50 percent discount instead of varying the discount based on other factors. It also took recruiter bonuses out of company earnings, not out of each sales recruit's earnings like the pyramid schemes.

This practice of taking commissions from the company side of the profit ledger is a small but grand statement of integrity. This kind of adherence to a philosophy was the most important business strategy in her overall compensation program. It clearly sent a message to her employees that Ash would run a business that had principles to which everybody would be held accountable.

The company also developed specific guidelines for its salespeople. Emphasis at home parties was on teaching, rather than selling, and the number of guests was held at no more than six. Delivery and payment on the spot were required, and beauty consultants could not purchase from the company on credit. Mary Kay also limited its product line so that salespeople would be knowledgeable about each product.

These insightful market positionings and practices were consistent with her rock-solid foundation that was based on one simple principle: the Golden Rule.

Unlike many sales companies, Mary Kay did not limit sales territories. Beauty consultants could recruit other consultants from anywhere in the world. The company also initiated an incentive program that included the use of a pink Cadillac. This famous prize was established in 1967 when a pink Cadillac was awarded to the top sales director. Annual conventions were held to recognize achievement, a practice that quickly became an important public relations event.

MODERN PARALLEL: ADAM SMITH, TWITTER COMMUNITY CHOREOGRAPHY (DANCE THEATER WORKSHOP)

Let's start off with an explanation of what Twitter is: Twitter is a way to send an instant message to everyone in the world instead of just one person. As a result of all that information being out in the open, it becomes a constant data stream of information about what people are talking about. Search Twitter for "innovation," for example, and you'll see thousands of results within the past few days.

The real genius of Twitter is that its creators left the software open to outside developers. They acknowledged that they weren't sure how people would use Twitter, so they left it to the masses to determine its potential. Like Mary Kay and her intentional decision not to limit sales territories, Twitter took down all boundaries that would prevent its service from becoming widespread.

As a result, thousands of different programs have been built using Twitter, and more continue to be built. Microsoft's Bing search engine incorporated Twitter data into its search results from day one. And individual Twitter users created the language of Twitter posts—"@" to denote a person's Twitter name, "D" for a direct message, and "RT" for "retweet," or a copy of someone else's Twitter message, giving that person credit for the text.

Some of the most unique uses of Twitter come from the unlikeliest of sources. One such source is New York's Dance Theater Workshop, or @dancetworkshop on Twitter.

It was autumn in New York in 2008, and the American economy was in shambles. Due to the prevalence of the financial district, New York City was hit particularly hard by the collapse of the stock market.

On West Nineteenth Street, a small, nonprofit dance theater was struggling. The revenue at Dance Theater Workshop (DTW) was down, and paid capacity at shows was at 58 percent for the year. DTW wasn't attracting the press, participation, or viewership of the videos it posted online, all the things it needed to stay afloat. Something had to change.

It was at this time that Twitter started to explode. Five hundred thousand Twitter profiles had been created by November 2008, and thousands more were being added every day. Even though most people had no idea what it was or how to use it, everyone was talking about it.

DTW's Adam Smith had recognized the potential of Twitter early on and had been tweeting from the DTW account to give a voice and personality to the organization. Already @dancetworkshop had a few hundred followers, but most of the interaction was one way: Smith would post a tweet and would hope that people would read it.

Smith decided to change that. With the help of performer and PR manager Jillian Sweeney, he essentially created a new form of dance using the Twitter platform. He called it Twitter Community Choreography (TCC).

TCC works as follows: On a Tuesday, Smith will tweet from DTW's Twitter account, asking for a dance move. Anyone can respond. Sometimes the request is broad, and sometimes it's more specific, like a one-word action or an animal name. The next day, he compiles the list of movements into a comprehensive, chronologically ordered list. Over the next week, he meets with the performer to discuss the dance (rarely do they reorder or drop any of the requested moves). The dancer then performs the dance on film. After editing it for fluidity, shape, and context, Smith posts it online for the world to see.

Smith's genius: He crowd-sourced dancing. He created interaction where there was none before.

The results have been nothing short of spectacular, both quantitatively and quantifiably. The first TCC received 13 moves. In October 2009, one TCC received 40. Watch one of the videos at www.dancetheater workshop.org and you can see the beauty of these dances. While you might think that 40 tweets from 40 different people would result in a disjointed, jerky dance, the performances actually have a raw, natural beauty to them.

The buzz around Twitter Community Choreography has put Dance Theater Workshop in the public eye. People who might otherwise have no interest in dance are intrigued by the concept. Where else can you send the name of an animal to a stranger and have a dance move created specifically for you, viewable online by hundreds of people?

Partially as a result of TCC (and other adaptations), Dance Theater Workshop has seen a huge amount of growth in paid attendance despite an economy that's rougher than before. Attendance currently stands around 80 percent of capacity for the year, up from 58 percent in 2008. That's the highest paid capacity over the past five years. The unique choreography has been the focus of numerous tech and dance blogs, as well as *Dance* magazine and social networking conferences.

Twitter Community Choreography has taken a form of expression as old as humankind and merged it with the latest in communication technology. Mary Kay would be proud of the way Dance Theater Workshop has redefined the philosophy of dance.

■ ■ ■

In the first full year of operation, Mary Kay Cosmetics sales totaled $198,514 and the company had 318 consultants. Soon, more office space was needed, and Mary Kay moved to a three-office headquarters with a training room and warehouse space for a total of 5,000 square feet. Within two years, Mary Kay had about 850 beauty consultants selling its beauty products.

Ash considered franchising to reach a wider market but decided against it. Instead, in 1967, the company went public and used the proceeds from the IPO to fund its expansion. Mary Kay Cosmetics was the first company on the New York Stock Exchange chaired by a woman.

The decision not to franchise was consistent with her desire to keep a simple philosophy intertwined into her daily operations. Although not impossible, it is much more difficult to achieve this under a franchise system, particularly when your greatest assets are the people who represent the company. In other words, when the real goods are the people and not an inanimate product like a pizza, it is easier to control that through tight corporate guidelines versus franchises that, by definition, are independently owned businesses.

For the next decade and a half, sales grew at an average of 28 percent per year. Between 1974 and 1978, however, sales slowed. To revive them, the company increased compensation rates for consultants. Sales rates once again rose and ranged from 29 percent to 82 percent growth for the next four years.

As sales grew, so did the company's need for space, so in 1969 a new 275,000-square-foot manufacturing facility was built in Dallas. A few years later, four regional distribution centers were constructed, and in 1977 a new eight-story headquarters building opened in Dallas. By 1993, the Mary Kay manufacturing facility was the size of three football fields. It also became an FDA-registered drug manufacturing facility, allowing the company to manufacture and distribute over-the-counter drugs such as sunscreen and acne treatment products.

These growth strategies would have been very difficult to execute under a franchised business model; consequently Ash's strategy to remain corporate proved to be a key element in the company's continued success.

The 1980s brought a reduction of growth as employment opportunities for women grew and more of them entered the full-time workforce. Between 1983 and 1985, Mary Kay's contingent of sales consultants was cut in half to 100,000. Sales fell from $323 million to $260 million. Fewer women were available to sell the products and fewer were at home to buy them.

THE LESSON: THE POWER OF INCENTIVES

Most businesspeople think they understand incentives. Dangle a bonus in front of someone, and the quality and quantity of their work will immediately improve. That's how it works.

Dan Pink, author of *A Whole New Mind* and *Drive,* begs to differ. Based on quantitative research from studies in behavioral economics, he proves that the best way to motivate and inspire creativity is not to offer cash bonuses and incentives. In fact, those types of incentives actually hurt some types of performance, especially creative problem solving.

The example Pink uses involves a study by Sam Glucksberg involving a group of students. The students are divided into small groups and are given a box of matches, a candle, and a few thumbtacks. They're told to find a way to affix the candle to the wall such that it doesn't drip on the floor, and they're timed to see how fast they can figure it out.

The twist is that some of the students are given a cash reward if they finish within the top 25 percent of the overall times, and the other students are offered no reward. Guess which group figures out the puzzle faster? The *non*-incentivized group, by nearly three and a half minutes. (The solution to the puzzle, by the way, is to use the actual box that the matches came in—most people don't see the box as something that can be used, at least for a few minutes).

The somewhat stunning results here indicate that incentives and bonuses actually stunt thinking and block creativity. Creative people— *innovative* people—need time and space to develop their ideas. Put a $1,000 bonus and a tight deadline in front of an employee, and maybe they'll come up with a decent short-term idea. But give that same employee the ability to work on their own projects on the company dime and time, just as Google does, and you might get the next Gmail.

The key point here is that you need to gear a strategy to specific types of employees for motivating and empowering innovation. Ash's strategy of offering cash bonuses and trips to Hawaii clearly worked for her sales team. How will you empower innovation among your employees?

■ ■ ■

The cosmetics market was highly competitive going into the 1990s, and industry growth was expected to hover only around the rate of inflation. Mary Kay Cosmetics, however, was looking to the overseas market for its greatest growth. It had been steadily adding foreign subsidiaries since 1971 when it opened its first international subsidiary in Australia. Mary Kay opened subsidiaries in Canada in 1978, Argentina in 1980, Germany in 1986, Mexico and Thailand in 1988, Taiwan in 1991, and Spain in 1992.

The 1990s also ushered in an increase in sales largely due to the inducements of larger commissions and bonuses. More consultants, however, were part-timers. Nearly 70 percent of the consultants had other jobs, whereas prior to the IPO, only 33 percent of the sales force had held other jobs.

Ash's ability to re-create the employment structure of the company during the cultural changes that were occurring during this time period allowed her to revamp her sales force several times. These management decisions would have been increasingly difficult under a franchise structure because she would have had less direct control over the employment base.

Mary Kay Cosmetics was included in both the 1984 and 1993 editions of "The 100 Best Companies to Work for in America." In 1993, Mary Kay also became a Fortune 500 company. The company surpassed $1 billion in retail sales in 1992, distributing more than 200 products through a sales force of more than 250,000 consultants in 19 countries. By 1993, the company had more than 300,000 salespeople in the United States and abroad, selling to nearly 20 million customers. More than half its national sales directors had earned more than $1 million during their Mary Kay careers, and the company was awarding nearly $38 million in prizes every year.

Ash was a pioneering woman in her day in America, but her company would become an international player as well. Her business philosophy was based on a universal truth that would also drive the company to becoming a worldwide brand.

Beauty consultants in many international markets distributed products made in the United States, but some Mary Kay products were produced in foreign countries for sale in those countries. Some foreign governments required that products be manufactured locally, whereas in other countries the duties on imports were so high that only local production would make the products affordable. Samples of all Mary Kay products made overseas were sent to the United States for testing.

By 1993, Mary Kay Cosmetics also had representatives in Bermuda, Brunei, Chile, Guatemala, Malaysia, New Zealand, Norway, Singapore, Sweden, and Uruguay. The company was considering foreign expansion options, including acquiring a manufacturing plant in Europe. Mary Kay's most important expansion that year was its entrance into Russia. Within two years, the company's Russian operations were pulling in $25 million in revenues.

The company's expansion into Asia was even more important to the company's growth in the mid-1990s. Mary Kay had developed very successful operations in Taiwan since it began operating there in 1991. By 1995, the company was generating revenues of $29 million there and anticipated even greater growth as Taiwan lowered its duty rate. The company moved into Japan in 1994 and China in 1995. Both countries were difficult to enter: Japan because the company had to reformulate most of its products to meet strict regulations, and China because of the complicated politics that had to be negotiated.

THE LESSON: THE POWER OF KEEPING THE FAITH DURING UPHILL BATTLES

No matter how good your product is, when you try to expand to be a national or global company, you're going to face numerous uphill battles and barriers. Language, politics, perception, taxes, tariffs, laws . . . these are all things that can get in the way of your company being successful.

Sometimes you have to pick and choose your battles. But if you know that you'll be successful in a specific market, you need to have the patience to stick with it until you find solutions for all the issues that arise. Have faith in your product and your company. If you truly believe in it, then you know that it's your duty to give everyone in the world the opportunity to purchase it.

■ ■ ■

By 1993, Mary Kay had become the best-selling brand of facial skin care and cosmetics in the United States, with wholesale sales of more than

$735 million. In addition to its financial success, the company still was considered an outstanding employer, making the lists of both the Fortune 500 and "The 100 Best Companies to Work for in America." Two years later, the company had surpassed $950 million in wholesale sales and was the best-selling skin care and cosmetics brand for the third year running.

Nice guys may finish last, but good people can certainly succeed. Ash would become the living example of faith in action.

In 1995 Mary Kay Ash retired from her position as chairman because of ill health. Although she retained the title of chair emeritus, by the following year Ash had withdrawn entirely from the company's operations. Given Ash's charismatic leadership, many questioned the effect her retirement would have on the company.

Yet in 1996 Mary Kay experienced its tenth consecutive year of record sales, with wholesale sales topping the $1 billion mark. In 1997 Mary Kay was the best-selling brand of facial skin care and color cosmetics in the United States, its fifth consecutive year to achieve that standing. That same year the company expanded into the Ukraine and the Czech Republic, and the following year into Brazil.

International operations remained an important source of growth for Mary Kay in the late 1990s. The company's prospects varied widely from country to country. Mary Kay's top-selling international subsidiary, Mary Kay Mexico, saw a 56 percent increase in revenues in 1997 over the year before. In 1998, after 10 years in operation, the subsidiary held 9 percent of the local cosmetics market. Between 1995 and 1998 the sales force grew 233 percent.

Mary Kay hoped to see similar success with its operations in China, but was thwarted by the Chinese government in 1998. That year China announced a ban on direct sales, sending the burgeoning operations there of Avon, Amway, and Mary Kay into a tailspin. Mary Kay was forced to abandon its traditional sales plan and enter the retail market to continue selling in that country. Despite this setback, the company entered the Hong Kong market in 1999, notwithstanding its reversion to Chinese rule that year.

Again, the company benefited from the corporate structure that it had adopted decades ago because it could easily convert its sales strategy from direct marketing to traditional retail sales.

The company celebrated its 35th anniversary in 1998 with the introduction of a white GMC Jimmy sport utility vehicle to its sales incentive plan. That year Mary Kay was named once again to *Fortune* magazine's list of "The 100 Best Companies to Work for in America."

Ash started the Mary Kay Ash Charitable Foundation in 1996. The organization is a nonprofit establishment that provides funding for research into cancers affecting women and is dedicated to putting an end to violence against women by supporting women's shelters and educational programs.

The story of Mary Kay Cosmetics shows that with a good product, a great philosophy, and a lot of faith, you can make a difference for millions of people around the world.

Chapter 8

INSIGNIFICANCE

Dr. Lonnie Johnson
Super Soaker (Hasbro)

To a nuclear engineer who holds over 50 patents and is recognized as one of the finest inventors in the world, a summertime toy may seem insignificant. To millions of kids who are eagerly waiting for summer fun to begin, a Super Soaker is priceless.

Dr. Lonnie Johnson is a former NASA nuclear engineer who began his career after graduating from Tuskegee University in Alabama in 1974. Johnson became an engineer at the Oak Ridge National Laboratory. He represents the importance of having the vision of a child. So many of the great innovators were childlike in their thirst for knowledge and their simple application of technology. Walt Disney and Steve Jobs come to mind as truly imaginative people who also possessed a simplicity to their visions. Johnson is a great example of seeing something that most people would never recognize, but millions have benefitted from: good, wholesome fun.

After his stint at the Oak Ridge Lab, he joined the Nuclear Power Safety Section at the Air Force Weapons Laboratory in Albuquerque, New

Mexico. In 1979, Johnson moved to the NASA Jet Propulsion Laboratory in Pasadena, California, where he became a senior systems engineer and worked on the *Galileo* mission to explore Jupiter.

He remained intellectually restless, and after a short stay he came back to the Air Force in 1982, where he became an advanced space systems requirement officer at Strategic Air Command headquarters in Omaha, Nebraska. Later he became chief of the Data Management Branch SAC Test and Evaluation Squadron at Edwards Air Force Base in California.

Because of his outstanding contributions, he was awarded the Air Force Achievement Medal and the Air Force Commendation Medal on two different occasions. But this curious scientist had many more innovations in store, one of which would become part of the summer tradition of playing with water guns.

While in the military, Johnson was tinkering with another revolutionary rocket force, a self-pressurized water gun. The idea behind what he initially named "Power Drencher" was actually derived from some work Johnson was doing on a heat pump that used water instead of Freon. He hooked up the model of the pump to his bathroom sink at his home. He discovered that he could shoot water across the bathroom with exceptional power.

Others may have seen this as a nuisance that merely made a mess to clean up. But Johnson saw value in this apparently insignificant turn of events. He recognized that this force could be used for good, specifically for the enjoyment of his young daughter. So he made a working prototype and allowed his daughter to play with it with her friends. To their delight and amazement, this was the coolest water gun in the neighborhood.

THE LESSON: THE POWER OF IMPRACTICALITY

Is a device that shoots water 20 feet or so practical? Is it useful? Does it serve a purpose?

No, no, and no. But that's okay. Not every new invention needs to save the world. Not every new web site needs to have a billion users. Not every innovative service needs to revolutionize the industry.

It's okay for something to be impractical. The next time you come up with a cool idea and think, "This is so much fun, but it's useless," think twice before moving on. You might just have the next Super Soaker, something that has brought joy to many a family.

■ ■ ■

Johnson realized that he did not have the resources or the manufacturing capability to produce the gun, but he understood the value of a patent and the potential of licensing his invention to a toy company. However, sometimes, even when you have the right vision and plan, reality has a way of getting in the way.

At the time, the water guns on the market were all motorized. These guns were rather expensive and were uncomfortable because of the combination of motors and water. Johnson's design was far superior because it relied on air pressure and arm pumping for pressurizing the firing chamber. This design was safer and more effective.

Johnson's journey to find a suitable licensing partner is itself a lesson about the twists and turns, the positives and pitfalls of licensing. However, in the end, as we will see, the path did in fact pay off.

The initial company interested in Johnson's innovation could be classified as the right company at the wrong time. The Daisy Company, known for its air rifles and BB guns, seemed like a natural fit. Unfortunately, the company was struggling with a restructuring process. This led to the creation of several management teams and consequently was not a very good environment for developing a revolutionary new toy gun. Because of the starts and stops, the company and Johnson were never successful at consummating a long-term licensing agreement.

Choosing a quality licensing partner is a key variable in successfully getting a new invention to market. Johnson struggled to find a suitable manufacturer that had both the capability and the financial capacity to undertake his project.

In 1987, he returned to the Jet Propulsion Laboratory (JPL), where he worked on the Mars *Observer* project and was the fault protection engineer during the early stages of the *Cassini* (Saturn) project. He was responsible for ensuring that single-point spacecraft failures would not result in loss of the mission. During his nine-year career with JPL, he received multiple achievement awards from NASA for his work in spacecraft system design. But being a determined inventor as well, he kept his dream alive regarding his revolutionary water gun.

He contacted a toy company called Entertech and arranged a meeting in their California office. By this time, Johnson had also invented some other toys to complement his water gun. During the presentation of his various toy concepts he explained that he had a water gun that could outperform Entertech's current motorized gun. This claim got the company's attention and soon an agreement was forged with Johnson to develop the water gun.

Unfortunately, the company never made it. Entertech filed for bankruptcy before the toy could go into production, and Johnson took back his innovative design. He had to start all over again to find the right licensing partner. But this apparent disappointment gave Johnson a chance to make a major refinement to his already stellar design.

During this process, Johnson designed and engineered several proto-type improvements to make the gun easier to manufacture. He decided to incorporate a blow-molded bottle on the gun as a pressure vessel. At the time, a common process in the toy industry was to use injection-molding toy components and glue them together. This approach was unreliable for use in constructing pressure vessels. Johnson's creation of a blow-molded bottle as a pressure vessel for the gun was the most important innovation that made the gun squirt powerful streams of water while keeping costs down through viable mass production.

THE LESSON: THE POWER OF ORGANIC DESIGN

Many times, inventions pave their own way to market by introducing unintended changes in the design process. In other words, innovation tends to push new limits on all aspects of development. As in the case of the Super Soaker, the initial innovation was from battery-operated water guns to self-propulsion, but what really moved the project along was innovation of the manufacturing process due to the new need to hold excessive amounts of pressurized water. Of course, this led to the use of blow-molded plastics, instead of injection-molded plastics, which meant much less expensive molds for the plastic. Secondary innovation is something that often creates the real opportunities.

■ ■ ■

In March 1989, Johnson met with Myung Song, president of Larami, at his Philadelphia office. Johnson took the improved water gun and shot a stream of water across the room, which astounded Larami's president. A contract was quickly put together and Larami assigned the project to Bruce D'Andrade to develop tooling for large-scale manufacturing. D'Andrade configured the gun components for manufacturing using injection-molded parts and added a "pinch trigger valve" in place of the original valve used by Johnson. The pinch trigger valve was used for less than three years, after which Larami returned to the use of valves that were more like the gun originally designed by Johnson.

While Super Soaker made its debut in 1991, improvements to the design and other aspects of water blaster technology did not stop then. Since its first release, numerous new developments and technologies have been added to the Super Soaker brand name. Johnson's top-mounted, blow-molded bottle became an icon that made this revolutionary water gun identifiable as the Super Soaker.

It is safe to say that any kid born after 1991 knows about the Super Soaker. I know my gang of eight kids have experienced countless hours of enjoyment with the many versions of Super Soakers that have been a part of our summers.

Through the years, Johnson has remained involved in the creative aspects of the Super Soaker product line. He has erected a full product development facility staffed with engineers and industrial designers from the Georgia Institute of Technology. He is able to create new products from prototype sketches all the way through to full-scale manufacturing. He has even created and tooled high performance compressed air rockets for Estes.

Lonnie Johnson is also responsible for many other developments, both toy- and non-toy-related. He has earned over 40 patents and continues to invent in the realms of thermo- and fluid-dynamics as well as toys. In addition to ongoing controls work for NASA, Johnson and his company are developing an improved home radon detector, a rechargeable battery, and a heat pump that uses water instead of Freon, among other projects.

Lonnie Johnson has won numerous honors for his success in inventing and entrepreneurship, and his constant encouragement of young people to invent. He is a legendary businessman and public figure in his hometown of Marietta, Georgia, whose mayor declared February 25, 1994, "Lonnie G. Johnson Day" in his honor—and, thanks to the Super Soaker, he is a hero to kids nationwide.

Most of all we see the very jagged road of innovation and licensing. For many people the disappointments would be too much to bear, but for Lonnie Johnson, each hurdle was simply a challenge that presented itself and inspired him to improve his design. His story is significant because it demonstrates two key aspects of innovation. First, the innovation is not an achievement, but a spectrum of achievements that must be managed throughout the life of an invention. Second, the process of licensing a patent is a simple concept that becomes increasing complex because of the importance of choosing the right partner to fully commercialize the product.

Thanks to Lonnie Johnson, we have a very successful example of how the innovation path can be traveled by an individual inventor who has the vision and determination to stay the course.

MODERN PARALLEL: PATRICK LOCKLEY, SIX BY SIX GALLERY

Sometimes the smallest pieces of art can make the biggest difference.

The year was 2008, and Patrick Lockley and his wife were running a successful gallery in New York City, along with a boutique printing company called Paper Slam. Many of their customers were individuals and collectors, but others were companies that provided a steady stream of business. The Lockleys often found themselves overwhelmed with the work flow and phone calls.

Then the economy came crashing down. By November, the Lockleys were waiting for the phone to ring. Customers were putting a hold on discretionary spending, and the gallery was starving for business.

The Lockleys realized that they needed a way to catalyze business in an economy that could be down for a while. During some intense brainstorming incorporating a "use what we have" mantra, they came up with the idea that they should use an extra storefront space they had recently acquired as a place to implement a new concept: the Six by Six Gallery.

The concept is brilliant in its simplicity: Use an existing space, ask artists (especially local ones) to contribute six-inch-by-six-inch works of art for a small submission fee, and hold monthly events to build buzz around the idea. Because of their bare-bones approach, the submission fees alone covered the cost of start-up.

They didn't use traditional marketing methods. Rather, the concept itself encouraged word-of-mouth marketing. It doesn't take a lot of time or resources to create a 6×6 piece of art—only a desire to create art and the effort to complete a piece. Additionally, the Lockleys were offering artists an 80 percent cut of the sales price (as opposed to the traditional 50/50 split), and it doesn't take a lot of money to buy a piece of art that size—prices are as low as $50. People who previously couldn't afford fine art or those who were stifled by the poor economy now had the opportunity to bring an original work into their homes.

The concept got people talking, word spread, and soon magazines, newspapers, and blogs were reporting about the Six by Six Gallery. By the time they had their first opening on October 2, 2009, people were lining up on the sidewalk in both directions.

Over 500 artists have become involved in Six by Six so far, and the Lockleys expect the concept to continue to grow. Overall, this is the perfect example of a brilliant adaptation in a tough economy.

Chapter 9

PARADOX

Jack Crawford Taylor
Enterprise Rent-A-Car

t is always fun to write about your hometown heroes. Jack Crawford Taylor is one of those. Like my father, Taylor was a World War II veteran, a fighter pilot, who would buck the system and turn an industry on its head. Enterprise would go against the grain to build a business battleship that is strong and standing tall today.

At the time that Taylor was looking to create a car rental business, the industry of rental cars was concentrated at airports during the growth of air travel. The industry grew even more after WWII, because of the growing popularity of air travel for business purposes. Hertz had anticipated this trend by opening a rental facility at Chicago's Midway Airport in 1932. Avis is credited with being the first company to do airport-focused rentals as its main source of business. The company's founder, Warren Avis, was a former Army pilot, and focused almost all its business toward airports and the surrounding areas.

Instead of following the existing competition in the growing industry, Jack Taylor would use a paradoxical strategy to outmaneuver and outservice his competition.

The predictable growth strategy would have been to set up his business at an airport. Clearly, the future of air travel was just beginning and there would be further need for quality suppliers of cars.

Instead, Taylor would utilize his talents and employ paradoxical thinking to develop Enterprise Rent-A-Car Company, the largest rental car company in North America with a strategy that was developed out of foresight and necessity.

In 1957, Taylor was gainfully employed at a local Cadillac dealer in St. Louis, Missouri. Before long he discovered that he had a desire to be an entrepreneur. Taylor occasionally came into contact with Cadillacs leased out of Chicago by a Greyhound subsidiary. Struck by the apparent ease and convenience of leasing an automobile, he investigated the business and found that the numbers looked promising. Taylor persuaded his boss to set up a leasing business, taking a 50 percent pay cut for a 25 percent share in the new business known as Executive Leasing Company. In a walled-off section of a body shop at the dealership in St. Louis, that branch of the company began with a fleet of seven vehicles. The company initially focused on long-term leasing, but Taylor began to examine the potential for short-term car rentals, entering this field in 1962.

The company had humble beginnings, but Taylor had a good eye for talent. He assigned a couple of young men, Don Ross and Doug Brown, to help him run the company. Don was a young enthusiastic kid who had just joined the company and Doug was going to St. Louis University at night and working his way through college. At Enterprise, Taylor gave them the task of increasing sales. Brown and Ross devised a strategy to call on insurance companies and focused on the AAA Auto Club of St. Louis, one of the major insurers in town. His strategy was to offer a better deal to the insurance companies so that instead of giving their customers an allowance, they would just provide a car. This strategy not only worked, but it also established a whole new industry, the insurance replacement business, that would become the basis for the company's expansion. Ironically, Jack Taylor loved the leasing business and but wasn't particularly comfortable with the rental business. But he gave clear instructions to the two young men: Pursue the business as long as you do not compromise the cultural benchmarks of the company.

It paid for Enterprise to think big. Instead of going to individual consumers, Enterprise went right to the top—the insurance companies. Innovative targeting like this immediately launched Enterprise onto the rental car scene.

Now, more than 40 years later, Doug Brown, now retired from Enterprise, is pursuing another paradoxical endeavor. He has established the first Habitat for Neighborhood Business in conjunction with St. Louis University to inspire, guide, and provide entrepreneurial and innovational opportunities and facilities in the inner city of St. Louis.

Don Ross is the current vice chairman of Enterprise.

Innovation many times is the result of arriving at a similar place, but taking a distinctly different route to find a better way. Enterprise is a good example of this. The Enterprise strategy was to largely avoid the higher-margin, highly competitive travel segment dominated by such companies as Hertz, Avis, and National. Instead, it took a path much less traveled as it began to develop a niche that was barely noticed by the major companies. This market included the temporary need for cars to replace ones that have been stolen, have been in an accident, were in need of a mechanical repair, or for a special occasion, such as a brief business trip. However, clearly the target customers were insurance adjusters and agents. The famous donuts delivered in a custom box with the Enterprise logo was a staple of the grassroots marketing program delivered to this customer base on a regular basis.

In 1969, the company branched out of St. Louis, opening an office in Atlanta, Georgia. Offices in Florida and Texas soon followed. To do so, however, a name change was in order because the Executive name was not available for use in some markets. The inside story is that the company principals weren't in love with the name anyway, but they did adore their logo. In order to preserve the brand look, they devised a very sophisticated naming search: They looked up words in the dictionary that started with the letter E and had about the same number of letters as *executive*. They settled on *enterprise*, which Taylor also liked because this was the name of a battleship he had served on in World War II. Brain surgery? Not quite. Brilliant? Absolutely!

Unlike the competition, Enterprise had an image and a way of doing business that reflected the discipline of a battleship. From the very neat appearance of the employees to the systematic way of doing business, the image of the *U.S.S. Enterprise* is a very good analogy to the operations of the business.

Taylor's national expansion got off to an excellent start in the early 1970s by targeting garage and body shop owners and persuading them to send their customers to Enterprise while their cars were in the shop. Motorists in the 1970s were so accustomed to freedom of movement that they could hardly live a day without a car, and drivers stranded while a car was being repaired were often happy to pay Enterprise's relatively low daily rate. This rate was much lower than the airport-based rental companies' rates. Business improved even more in the early 1970s when a judicial precedent was set requiring casualty insurers to compensate insured motorists for economic loss due to being without a car. This is a very good example of when preparation meets opportunity. Enterprise was there to take advantage of the situation.

THE LESSON: HELPING PEOPLE AT THE POINT OF NEED

Enterprise did something very clever by providing a service at the point of need—at the time when people are most helpless. Instead of creating a new need, they simply recognized an existing need and swooped in to help.

Some companies take advantage of customer vulnerabilities. Not Enterprise. Think about the number of times you feel vulnerable, even just in your day-to-day life. And think of the services that help you feel less vulnerable. You can do some good in the world by stepping in where no one has.

One of trademark developments of the early 1970s came from a branch manager in Orlando, who began offering customers a free ride to the rental office. This service was quickly introduced throughout the growing Enterprise system, beginning the tradition that would be immortalized in the well-known company slogan, "We'll pick you up." In choosing to go above and beyond the call of duty and creating a catchy tagline for it, Enterprise cemented itself in consumer's minds as *the* rental company that comes to get you wherever you are. Later, when other companies added the same service, it was too late— Enterprise was ahead of the game.

■ ■ ■

Enterprise dominates the local segment of the automobile rental market, catering largely to those consumers who need to rent. The replacement car niche tends to be resilient in times of recession, and its traditionally fragmented nature has allowed Enterprise plenty of room for growth. In addition to its rental car and fleet services businesses, Enterprise also has a car sales unit and a rental truck operation, the latter largely offering trucks for replacement and supplemental purposes to commercial businesses.

The energy crisis of 1974 hampered rental car expansion for a short period. Although Enterprise continued to show a profit, the difficult economic conditions inspired the company to diversify. In addition, the company had become so adept at recruiting and training young talent, they had a personnel pool that was busting at the seams. In order to keep this talent in the company, they purchased Keefe Coffee Company, a provider of in-room coffee service to hotel guest rooms. This venture, in turn, started what became Enterprise Capital Group (ECG), which expanded through acquisitions during the 1970s. The next acquisition was Monogramme Confections, a candy maker selling hotels and businesses candies with customized wrappers bearing their own logo. Other additions to the ECG's Nonautomotive Group included another coffee service, Courtesy Coffee, and Crawford Supply, a service provider to correctional facilities.

THE LESSON: HOW TO KEEP EMPLOYEES
IN TOUGH TIMES

Enterprise teaches us a timely lesson here. The company had spent tons of time, money, and staff resources training employees into an elite corps of young talent—why waste all those sunk costs by laying off those same employees once the economy took a turn for the worse?

Instead of letting those employees go, Enterprise acquired new businesses so those employees could have something to do. And not just something to do—these were management positions in which their employees could continue to grow and improve.

In 2009, many companies don't have the cash to just acquire new companies. But some are finding ways to keep talented employees without sacrificing the profit line. Some companies offer employees unpaid time off (with benefits) called furloughs. Others offer reduced pay for a while. In what creative way will you keep your best talent when tough times strike?

Clearly, the most significant ingredient of Enterprise's success in all business segments was its emphasis on customer service. The "Customer Giveaway Account" was set up to allow any Enterprise Rent-A-Car employee to charge off items up to a certain limit in order to satisfy a customer. A motivated workforce was also crucial to the operation, and Enterprise instituted a variety of bonus plans that provided incentives to everyone from assistant branch managers on up. Customer service was further enhanced in 1980 with the opening of the National Reservation Center, which enabled customers to call a toll-free number to rent Enterprise vehicles nationwide.

■ ■ ■

One of the key differences between Enterprise and the other industry giants was that Enterprise chose not to franchise its operations. This provided Enterprise both a cost advantage and the ability to accept lower profits during difficult economic periods. But most importantly, it provided direct control of the operations, which is critical to the superior service advantage that Enterprise holds over its competitors.

THE LESSON: THE POWER OF NOT FRANCHISING

There is something to be said for franchising. But for many companies, intentionally choosing not to franchise may be the best option. This is particularly important when a company is trying to create and maintain a specific brand.

Franchising is certainly tempting—someone pays you a flat fee for hard work that you've already done. But before you go that route, think about the long term implications for your company. Will franchising help or hurt the overall brand? Will it expand your concept and company in a positive way, or will it dilute your big plans? And think about it from the customer perspective: If someone walks into another franchised store and then they later walk into your store, will the experience be confusing for them? Or will it solidify their belief in and support of your company?

Enterprise's growth, meanwhile, continued throughout the 1970s and accelerated in the 1980s, averaging a 27 percent increase annually between 1984 and 1990. A new threat was presented in the 1980s, when Hertz and National entered the home-city rental market. The business was vastly different from business and leisure travel rentals, and Hertz quickly found the profit margins to be too low. Hertz decided to pull out of the market by the end of the decade, and National's operations struggled to stay afloat. Enterprise, meanwhile, began cultivating a market called "discretionary rentals" in the late 1980s. Aimed at families visiting relatives, or kids coming home for the holidays, discretionary rentals offered cars at low prices.

■ ■ ■

In 1987, Enterprise Capital Group purchased a cellular telephone company. Enterprise Cellular added millions of dollars in revenue. The group's experience with an unprofitable frozen Mexican food subsidiary in the 1980s convinced Enterprise that its success was more closely related to giving superior customer service than to the quality of any specific product it handled. Future diversifications would be made with this in mind.

MODERN PARALLEL: ROBIN SLOAN, ROBIN WRITES A BOOK (VIA KICKSTARTER)

Robin Sloan started with a blog and a book idea. A month later, without using any traditional publishing methods, he had over $13,000 and a completed novella.

It all started with the idea that Robin wanted to create a relationship with an audience. A simple request. Robin's a great writer, so I'll let him explain the concept to you in his own words as sent to me when I asked him about his end goal:

> My goal is definitely to build an audience—a community. The biggest challenge facing new writers (or, you name it: new musicians, new artists) is getting attention. There's just so much good stuff out there; why should anybody spend any of their time, let alone their money, on yours? Cory Doctorow puts it nicely—in the context of people copying your work, he says: "The real threat isn't piracy. It's obscurity." And I think that's exactly right.
>
> So, I wouldn't call it an "end goal" because it's really all about building something over time—it's not like I'll be finished when this project is over. The idea is to build that base of attention and investment over time—build the group of people who are out there thinking, "Yeah, I dig this guy Robin's work, and I want to see what he does next"—project by project, person by person.

I discovered Robin's project on Kickstarter in October 2009. I had recently discovered Kickstarter myself (www.kickstarter.com). It's a new web site that allows people to fund creative projects by asking lots of people to contribute small amounts of money and get small rewards in return. A person might ask for gas money for a road trip to Yosemite, for example, so he could take pictures of the park with a special camera he invented. In return for some money, he'll offer a first-edition photo from the trip.

The projects vary greatly, but Robin's stood out because it was clear that he was trying something new and innovative. Every aspect of his Kickstarter page (www.kickstarter.com/projects/robinsloan/robin-writes-a-book-and-you-get-a-copy) was geared toward getting more books into the hands of more people. Not only did he want to grow an audience, but he wanted each dollar contributed to go as far as possible. Mass-ordering via print-on-demand companies like Lulu (the company Robin used) kept the cost of the books much lower than if Robin tried to sell them one by one.

He chose the following contribution levels:

Pledge $1 or more: Get a PDF copy of the book.

Pledge $3 or more: Get a PDF copy of the book plus behind-the-scenes updates.

Pledge $11 or more: Get a physical copy of the book.

Pledge $19 or more: Get a signed copy of the book.

Pledge $29 or more: Get a signed copy of the book with your name in the acknowledgments.

Pledge $39 or more: Get four copies of the book.

Pledge $59 or more: Have four copies of the book shipped internationally.

Note the economy of scale in the pledge levels. Robin created huge incentives for individuals to buy more than one copy of the book. In doing so, he's creating a grassroots movement behind the book *before anyone has read a word.*

Better yet, Robin created a story to tell. He let people in on the progress of the book as he was writing it. He was a talented enough writer to get published the traditional way, but he eschewed that route for this new method of production and distribution. And he promised his readers that they would receive the book in a truly unique, memorable way.

I received Robin's book on December 15, 2009. After opening the outside packaging, I discovered that the book inside was enclosed in a shiny, chromatic material. The effect was that the book had been sent from the future to my doorstep. As much as I adore the Amazon.com publishing, this was better by far.

Robin's innovative approach to publishing couldn't have come at a better time. When the world appears to be moving toward electronic books, he created value in the experience of holding a book in your hands.

The Kickstarter approach isn't the only way to incentivize the purchase of multiple books at once. Other authors do that too, most notably of late Gary Vaynerchuk's *Crush It!* experience (www.crushitbook.com). But Robin was looking at a completely different scale than a well-known author with an established audience like Vaynerchuk. Robin was seeking to reach people he had never met, friends of friends of friends, blog readers, and hopefully a few people like me who just stumbled onto his Kickstarter page.

In the end, he reached 570 backers, over 100 of them at the $39 and $59 levels. He raised over $13,000. What will Robin think of next? Stay tuned at www.robinsloan.com.

When you innovate, how will you build an audience?

By the early 1990s, the Enterprise Capital Group represented about 10 percent of Enterprise's revenues. Meantime, in 1989, the company changed its name to Enterprise Rent-A-Car Company to reflect what had become by far its largest business, with more than 500 offices and a fleet of more than 50,000 rental vehicles.

■ ■ ■

In 1989, Enterprise began advertising with an eye toward creating brand recognition of its service. With an initial television advertising budget of only about $5 million, Enterprise decided to strategically place its messages so that they would be seen by a demographically favorable group. The company limited its television sponsorship to one network—CBS—hoping to reach the older, upper-income audience watching *60 Minutes* and *Murder She Wrote*. The practice seemed to work for the company as Enterprise's revenues hit $800 million in 1990.

As the decade continued, Enterprise's second generation of leadership was looking optimistically to the future. The company was gaining strength while its competitors were trying to restructure and reshape their futures. Though successful competitors such as Action, Agency, and Chrysler's Snappy Car Rentals had crept into Enterprise's domain, none had the foothold in the market enjoyed by Enterprise.

Jack Taylor's son Andrew, president of the company since the early 1980s and chief executive officer since 1991, picked up where his father had left off. Under Andrew Taylor's guidance, Enterprise's level of customer service was not allowed to suffer through overly ambitious expansion, with growth proceeding at a pace dictated by the number of qualified managers available. Enterprise already operated in nearly all of the nation's top 100 market centers by 1992, and the company's successful recruitment and training programs promised no delays in growth. That year, revenues surpassed $1 billion for the first time. The company's leasing division took on the name Enterprise Fleet Services as it focused on serving business with small to midsized fleets.

THE LESSON: DICTATE GROWTH BASED ON YOUR EMPLOYEES

Andrew Taylor made a key decision for the future success of Enterprise: He based the pace of Enterprise's expansion on the number of qualified managers. He didn't dilute his brand and let customer service suffer. Instead, he continued with a highly successful training program, and when people were ready, he expanded the company.

Don't do this the other way around.

Enterprise's growth accelerated in the mid- to late 1990s. Revenues jumped to $2.46 billion by fiscal 1995 and then to $4.73 billion by 1999. By decade's end the rental fleet had reached half a million vehicles, which were offered through 4,000 offices worldwide. This growth was aided by an international push that saw the company open its first international office in Windsor, Ontario, in 1993 and then open its first office in Europe the following year in Reading, England. While the off-airport market remained Enterprise's core business—a sector in which it held as much as a 50 percent share of the U.S. market in the 1990s—the firm began encroaching on the sector still dominated by Hertz and Avis, opening its first on-airport location at the Denver

International Airport in 1995. By the end of the 1990s, Enterprise was renting vehicles at 95 of the top 100 airports in the United States; at about half of these it had counters in the airport terminal, while the remainder were served by nearby offices.

■ ■ ■

Meantime, Enterprise reached a milestone in 1996: It surpassed Hertz as the number one car rental company in the United States in terms of fleet size and number of offices. Enterprise also battled Hertz and other car rental companies over the use of the "We'll pick you up" line, which Enterprise had trademarked and had been using in advertising since 1994. The company reached an out-of-court settlement with Hertz over the matter in 1998.

International expansion continued in 1997 with the opening of offices in Ireland, Scotland, Wales, and Germany. In 1999, Enterprise launched its Rent-A-Truck business, which rented trucks for replacement and supplemental purposes to commercial businesses. That same year, the Taylor family split off Enterprise's nonautomotive businesses into a separate company, Centric Group.

Revenues stagnated in the post-9/11 travel downturn, but Enterprise fared better than its rivals, who saw their sales drop, because Enterprise continued to specialize more in the replacement car market, which held up better than the business and leisure travel markets. Revenues for fiscal 2002 were up just 3 percent, reaching $6.5 billion. By the end of 2002, Enterprise had 115 on-airport locations and had captured 3.3 percent of that market. Its five-thousandth rental location opened that year, and its rental fleet included more than 533,000 vehicles.

THE LESSON: BECOMING RECESSION-PROOF

Enterprise succeeded in the recession because it didn't rely much on travelers. When the economy goes south, traveling decreases. Enterprise was essentially impervious to such dips in the market because it wasn't reliant on tourism—it had its strongest market share in replacement cars, which people need regardless of the economy.

Is your business built on a foundation that is stable no matter the state of the economy? Is it based on need instead of frivolity? Is it based on everyday life instead of leisure and vacation expenses?

Enterprise acquired National Car Rental and Alamo Rent A Car in 2007. As a result of these acquisitions, Enterprise Holdings is the world's largest car rental company with more than 8,000 locations and more than 78,000 employees stationed throughout the world.

■ ■ ■

J.D. Power and Associates announced the 2009 Rental Car Satisfaction Study results, and three of the top four rankings went to the Enterprise Holdings portfolio of brands: Enterprise Rent-A-Car (ranking highest), National Car Rental (ranking second) and Alamo Rent A Car (ranking fourth).

The story of Enterprise, simply stated, recognizes the simple but rare ability to look at things not only from another perspective but also from an apparently contradictory perspective in order to achieve innovative success.

Chapter 10

LUCK

William Procter and James Gamble
Procter & Gamble

I t is one thing to marry for money, and quite another to marry for an employee. Alexander Norris took it a step further, two times over. The result of his innovative matchmaking would become the home products giant Procter & Gamble.

William Procter and James Gamble came from different countries but shared the same goal: to seek a new life in America. Procter was an Englishman who had lost his U.K. wool shop to burglary and fire. Gamble was an Irishman who came to America as a young boy when famine devastated Ireland. Procter was a candle maker by trade while Gamble was a soap maker. They had one key thing in common for old man Norris: They were both attracted to the Norris girls.

In unions approved (or set up) by Norris, each man took one of the daughters as his wife. Their insightful father-in-law saw the potential of these two lads and convinced them that two heads were better than one, even if one was English and the other Irish. But Mr. Norris had much more strategic plans than merely trying to get his two new family members to collaborate with each other. He recognized—and pointed out to his new family members—that both candles and soap had common ingredients, namely lye, animal fat, and wood ashes.

Soon Norris had his sons-in-law running a small shop in Cincinnati. Procter ran the store while Gamble handled the manufacturing process in the back room. The first manufacturing equipment consisted of a wooden kettle with a cast-iron bottom. Each morning, Gamble visited homes, hotels, and steamboats to retrieve scraps of meat and wood ash. He traded bars of soap for the scraps. In 1837, it was one of the first recycling operations in America.

Candles were the primary product of the new start-up and provided the young company a steady business. But Procter & Gamble was only one of many companies in this field, as candles were a staple product in America in the pre-Edison era. However, the company had some logistical advantages. First, it was located near the Ohio River, which helped expand the business by providing a waterway to ship products down the river. Second, the town of Cincinnati was well linked to eastern cities by the railroads. Thus, their strategic location solidified the business as a viable company.

THE LESSON: THE POWER OF LOCATION, LOCATION, LOCATION

It goes without saying that location can make the difference between a successful brick-and-mortar business and a failing one. With the abundance of modern infrastructure already in place—particularly in urban areas—a building may already be standing where you think your business has the best chance to succeed. Fortunately, there are modern systems to help you determine which area is the best fit for you and which lots are vacant or for rent.

One such system is ZoomProspector (www.zoomprospector.com), a Web-based platform for finding the optimal location for your brick-and-mortar business. Simply plug in a few parameters and output the results, and then filter them by available properties for rent or sale (if you don't want to erect a new building). You can even filter by demographics like education, unemployment rate, age, and population size.

Procter & Gamble got a little lucky with their location—but don't leave your business's success up to luck. Be smart about choosing your location.

■ ■ ■

Procter & Gamble has given meaning to the saying, "It's better to be lucky than good." This in no way takes away from its success but adds a dimension to it that many ventures never benefit from. Its first run of good fortune had to do with its famous trademark. It began as a simple cross mark that was placed on the boxes to help dockhands differentiate P&G shipments from those of other manufacturers. It was later modified by other, more creative dockhands who made it more distinguishable: a circle with a depiction of the man in the moon. This practice was not unusual in that time period because many workers in 1851 were illiterate, so symbols were used to simply identify the boxes so they could be shipped correctly. Procter & Gamble's simple marking was more attractive than most and became well known. After the symbol had established itself, William Procter enhanced it further by adding 13 stars to represent the 13 colonies. This mark became so popular that a competing company from Chicago attempted to copy it, but P&G sued and won. It was not until 1882 that the famous moon and stars logo was registered as a federal trademark.

THE LESSON: THE POWER OF A LOGO

Your company's logo isn't going to make or break the business. But it can have a powerful impact on customers' impression and memory of the company.

When Jamey Stegmaier's Web-based business, TypeTribe, was in the fledgling stages of development, Jamey hired a designer to create a logo and a wordmark (the *wordmark* is what your company name will look like when it's typeset). Typically this process involves a brainstorming session between the company and the designer, followed by color selection, a palette of various logo samples, and then some tweaks and finishing touches. Some companies pay hundreds of thousands of dollars for this process (which they call *rebranding* to justify the expense to their investors); in truth, for a small business, you can hire a designer to make a logo for less than $1,000.

Even if you're still developing your innovation, keep an eye out for logos that stand out and perfectly represent the company or product. Be mindful of iconic logos of huge companies like American Airlines, ESPN, Disney, and Pepsi (which updated its logo in 2009) as well as smaller companies with clean, effective logos such as Evernote (an application that helps you clip notes from practically everywhere) and Bistro 1689.

■ ■ ■

There is also a saying that, "The harder you work, the luckier you get," which applies to Procter & Gamble (P&G). With the country on the brink of the Civil War, cousins James Norris Gamble and William Alexander Procter were dispatched to New Orleans by their fathers to purchase large quantities of rosin, which is derived from pine sap and only available in the South. This strategic purchase solidified P&G manufacturing output during the war as their competitors fell short. In addition, the company innovated at the end of the war by experimenting with silicate of soda as a viable substitute. It later became a key ingredient in modern soap products.

As the railroads were making it easier for companies to ship products from coast to coast, Procter & Gamble was continuing to research and innovate with new products. Aiming for cost reduction without sacrificing quality, the company developed a new soap that achieved this objective. It was originally called white soap, but was soon rebranded as Ivory. It became an instant success and had a very unusual quality: It was the first soap that floated in water.

However, this unique and very marketable feature wasn't designed in the laboratory; rather, it happened in a much more curious fashion. One day during production, a machine operator forgot to turn off the mixing machine before he left for his lunch break. Upon his return, he noticed that the soap was still churning, which caused more air to be mixed into the product than normal. The product was packaged and shipped as usual, but it received an incredible response from consumers who were tired of fishing around in the bottom of the tub for sunken soap. Everybody wanted the soap that floats.

At first the company was confused by the response, but after the accident was confessed by the machine operator, Procter & Gamble quickly turned the mistake into one of the best marketing strategies of all time. Ivory soap would single-handedly be responsible for growing the company to the prime position in the industry.

MODERN PARALLEL: ALMA M. LUGTU, COVER MY BUM™

Walk down the aisles of any grocery store and you'll see hundreds of options for every product. Companies do everything they can to distinguish their products from their competitors'. Imagine a nine-teenth-century consumer making the choice between soaps: Given the option between a bar of soap that floats and one that doesn't (despite the similarities in scent, utility, and price), the average consumer would choose the one that floats in a bucket of water.

However, before Ivory was invented (or stumbled upon), if you had circulated a survey asking people what they wanted in a bar of soap, most respondents would specify a color, smell, or size they liked, because those were the variables available at the time (albeit on a much more limited scale than modern soaps). This same phenomenon happened during a study performed by psychophysicist Howard Moscowitz in the early 1980s (as detailed in Malcolm Gladwell's 2009 book *What the Dog Saw*).

Moscowitz was hired by Prego to determine the optimal type of Prego spaghetti sauce. At the time, there were very few varieties to choose from. For the study, Moscowitz created 45 different varieties of Prego. He went all over the country to test the 45 sauces, and when he compiled the results, it turned out that there were three types of spaghetti sauces that people really liked: plain, spicy, and extra chunky.

At the time, extra chunky spaghetti sauce wasn't sold in grocery stores. It was barely produced at all. Previous studies by Prego where they sat people down and asked them what they wanted in spaghetti sauce had revealed no interest in extra chunky sauce.

The lesson here is that people don't know what they want until you give it to them. That doesn't mean that consumers will like every brilliant innovation you have—just because *you* think it is brilliant doesn't mean that *they* will. And as is noted in Chapter 5, people generally don't respond well to companies, products, and especially web sites throwing a million different options at them in the hope that something sticks. Sometimes you just have to invent or innovate something that doesn't exist on the market—a soap that floats, a spaghetti sauce that doesn't drain through the noodles—and see if it's the thing that people unknowingly wanted all along.

A great modern example of this hails from a sport that didn't even exist when Ivory soap was created: the triathlon.

The term "triathlon" is somewhat ubiquitous; it refers to a combination of any three sports or tests of fitness. However, the word is most often used in reference to the Ironman Triathlon (circa 1978), which consists of a 2.4-mile swim followed by a 112-mile bike ride, topped off with a 26.2-mile run. It's three different marathons in a row, all three equal parts exhaustion and invigoration.

The first triathlon in 1978 included 15 contestants. Two decades later, a similar race hosted 1,500 athletes (out of 50,000 applicants). A few years later in 2002, the Jamba Juice Wildflower Triathlon in California included 7,000 entrants. An estimated 150,000 people competed in triathlons that year. Just four years later, more 320,000 people registered with USA Triathlon, the sport's governing body (registrations include annual or one-time registrations for single events).

Remarkably, despite such rapid growth early on, the sport continues to expand its membership. Part of the appeal is that there are various forms of the triathlon that cater to different audiences while still maintaining the consistency of the original Ironman. In fact, the most popular form is the sprint, a half-mile swim followed by a 12- to 18-mile bike ride, finished with a 3-mile run. The Ironman can take hours upon hours; conversely, people can finish the sprint version within an hour. (Despite the grueling nature of the Ironman, more than 88,000 people competed in that variety of the race alone in 2008.)

Not only does the sport's growth make it ripe for investment, but the type of people who compete in triathlons are typically very wealthy. Mediamark Research noted in 2005 that the average income of subscribers to *Triathlete* magazine was $155,000. In addition, triathletes tend to be "gearheads" who spend thousands of dollars on equipment for the three portions of the race. There are plenty of toys to help you get ready for a triathlon and perform at a high level during the event: special pools, bikes, outfits, shoes, heart monitors—the list goes on.

Despite all the technology that goes into a successful triathlete program, there is one simple yet crucial item that is grossly overlooked: the towel.

This is where cover my bum™ comes in.

A key part of a successful—and comfortable—triathlon is the transition from the swim to the bike. Riding 112 miles—or even just 16 miles—in a wet bathing suit is quite uncomfortable. Most athletes opt for a change in clothing. Whether you're competing for time or accomplishment, making that transition smooth is really important. And yet most athletes use a standard cotton towel to dry off and cover up while they change. It's heavy, it's bulky, it doesn't dry out easily, and as anyone who's tried to change clothes under a towel can attest, it doesn't always cover everything you need it to.

Alma M. Lugtu, a triathlete since 1999, realized this the hard way while training in Denver. After accidentally exposing herself several times, she decided enough was enough. There must be a better way.

Lugtu also realized that she wasn't alone in her frustrations. When triathletes dry off and change, they're sequestered in an area that's blocked off from spectators—but still completely visible. Picture hundreds, if not thousands, of wealthy gearheads struggling to dry themselves with cotton towels (often soaked with rain) and then cover themselves with those same towels. The image is almost comical.

So Lugtu set out to invent a better towel. She talked to other triathletes about hypothetical towels, but due to the lucrative nature of the business, she kept the concept secret until she filed a provisional patent. She researched various fabrics and different attachment methods to hold the towel secure while changing (to ensure that bums are covered), and she sewed the first prototype herself.

With the prototype and more exact drawings in hand, Lugtu began talking to fellow triathletes, swimmers, and race directors. Her idea was warmly received. In addition, due to a little luck, other types of athletes noticed the designs as well and mentioned that they'd like a version of the towel for their sports. One of these was a mountain biker who saw Lugtu's drawings as she spread them over her table at a coffee shop. Another was a friend who was hoping for a similar solution for changing while hiking and camping. Yet another person pointed out that the towel was perfect for surfers, who can be fined if they expose themselves while changing on the beach.

Although it seemed like luck at the time, Lugtu was putting herself in situations where the idea could be seen by many different types of athletes and the buzz for cover my bum could grow. It helps that she is outgoing—once she had her patent, she talked up a storm, and the interest in her idea was immediately evident.

Spurred by the positive feedback, Lugtu moved forward with a second round of prototypes. Again, backed by hard work, patience, and research, she found herself getting lucky with suppliers and manufacturers alike. She found a fabric supplier in China that would sell her 50 yards of microfiber (the industry standard is 500 to 1,000 yards). She also found a manufacturer in Denver to create the prototypes for free in exchange for Lugtu's extensive research about the triathlon field, as they were looking into putting some products on the market as well.

At the time of this writing, Lugtu is designing a third round of prototypes based on feedback from the previous versions. Her story is the only one in this book where the success of the innovation is yet to be known. It seems that cover my bum has the perfect storm of luck, demand, and buying power—it's just a matter of time until Lugtu puts the towel on the market and gives triathletes the chance to purchase the one piece of gear they never knew they wanted all along. Check it out at www.covermybum.com.

■ ■ ■

The Ivory brand also lent itself well to advertising, which was a frowned-upon practice at this time, usually reserved for companies with less than honorable reputations. But Ivory, with its pure image and built-in story, would overcome this cultural hurdle. The first advertising budget for this remarkable product was $11,000 in 1892 and the slogan was "99% Pure." This new practice of consumer marketing also convinced the company to begin an extensive quality control and testing program to ensure that they could back their claims with evidence. This became the cornerstone of the famed P&G research and product development program.

THE LESSON: THE POWER OF BARK AND BITE

Some companies produce a decent product and market it as if it's the best thing ever invented. Other companies produce truly amazing products but don't advertise them well. Then there are those rare instances where a company goes all out not only for quality, utility, and design, but also for how they get the word out about the product.

Which type of company do you want to build?

The incredible success of Ivory persuaded the company to build a new plant on the outskirts of Cincinnati called Ivorydale and to hire a chemist to lead a more extensive effort of research, innovation, and development. The company developed additional soaps geared toward industrial uses and continued to grow at a rapid pace.

■ ■ ■

This fast-growing business encountered labor problems, which resulted in many strikes over the next several years and had a negative impact on production at a time when the business was growing rapidly. This motivated the company to reexamine the whole approach to employee relations and resulted in a pioneering employee incentive and benefit program. Procter & Gamble experimented with several employee compensation and loyalty programs during the upcoming year and has been a consistent leader in the development of cutting-edge, innovative employee programs throughout its history.

THE LESSON: THE POWER OF EMPLOYEE LOYALTY

In Chapter 7 (Mary Kay Cosmetics and faith), we talked about how monetized incentives can actually stifle creativity at the workplace. In Chapter 6 (Hershey and failure), we discussed Barry-Wehmiller's methods for making employees feel like they're part of the big picture instead of just cogs in a machine. In Chapter 4 (Apple and intuition), we learned that Zappos offers to pay employees to quit after a short training period to weed out those who don't buy into the corporate philosophy.

Employees matter. Your employees will make or break your business.

Procter & Gamble realized this when it was almost too late. If it hadn't responded the way it did, the company may not exist today.

How can you compensate your employees and ensure their loyalty? It certainly depends on the type of company, but there are some universal truths to be gleaned for 2010 and beyond:

- Give employees time to be creative.
- Give employees space to be autonomous.
- Give employees projects that make them think.
- Give employees a platform to share their successes *and* shortcomings.
- Give employees an understanding of how they affect the bottom line.
- Give employees the resources they need to be efficient and comfortable.
- Give employees feedback and a way for them to give you feedback.

The ground rules of Procter & Gamble were firmly established by the two brothers-in-law who had been encouraged by their father-in-law to find a way to work together. Cooperation fortified with an insatiable appetite for innovation and complemented by incentives for employees is a formula that has produced results with incredible success for many decades.

■ ■ ■

The company developed a cadre of new products, including a revolutionary new cooking oil called Crisco in 1911. After applying the P&G marketing model of promotion and advertising, the product became a huge success.

William Procter and James Gamble never forgot the lesson they had learned many years before and made sure the company was well prepared for an ingredient shortage when World War I loomed on the horizon. They stockpiled raw ingredients so that the company would not have production problems during the war. Procter & Gamble introduced many new products and categories during the next two decades, including Ivory Flakes, Chipso Flakes for industrial laundries, Camay, Oxydol, and synthetic soaps.

THE LESSON: THE POWER OF FORESIGHT

Procter & Gamble had the foresight to stockpile raw materials well ahead of wartime shortages. This is a perfect example of how a great company emerged from tough times—it foresaw the tough times and was ready for them when they arrived.

Where do you foresee the 2008–2009 economic crisis going? Is it too late to stock up on commodities relevant to your innovation that may be lacking in the future? Many companies are betting that global oil shortages will push consumers to buy vehicles that run on alternative energy sources. Toyota bet on this years ago and is now reaping the profits with the Prius.

Where else do you see America and the rest of the world headed in the next few years? Where do you see your company in that time? How can you predict the future and act to align the two?

■ ■ ■

During the Great Depression, Procter & Gamble contributed several key innovations that would set the standard for business operations in the future. It began with the establishment of a distinct method for brand management. The concept was of one man, one brand that concentrated attention on a more individualized approach to running the various products within the company. This became the standard for almost all future consumer product companies in America.

Radio advertising became an effective vehicle for the company. Procter & Gamble, creator of the first floating bar of soap, pioneered a new soap concept that would become a cultural icon of America. This concept was called the *soap opera*. By 1939, there were 29 different soap operas on the radio; in total, they brought in over $9 million in marketing revenue (roughly $140 million in 2009 dollars).

THE LESSON: THE POWER OF DIVERGENT REVENUE STREAMS

The soap company created a type of TV show. The online superstore created the book of the future (Amazon and the Kindle). The movie giant created theme parks (Disney and Disneyland).

One of the boldest moves you can make is to diversify your revenue streams into areas that—at first glance—have nothing to do with your company. In the twenty-first century, an era of Web-based companies that have no revenue streams at all, such a move may be necessary for a company's survival.

Take Burnie Burns and *Red vs. Blue,* a comedy series that uses creative footage from the *Halo* video game instead of traditional animation. As soon as the series launched online in 2003 with a few friends, millions of people were downloading the episodes every week.

Burns must have been swimming in cash, right? Unfortunately that wasn't the case. *Red vs. Blue* was free to download and view. The result was that each episode was easily shared, resulting in something that everyone within a certain niche of geeks was talking about. But Burns wasn't seeing any revenue despite having an audience the size of an average cable network show.

Rather than try to charge people a small amount to download the show, which may have resulted in the loss of a huge percentage of viewers, Burns and his friends came up with a completely unrelated source of revenue: T-shirts.

T-shirts give consumers a way to declare allegiance to something they're passionate about, and once someone puts one on, it's free advertising for the company in question. With print-on-demand companies like Zazzle and CafePress, you can make a profit on the first sale instead of stocking up on shirts that you may never sell. And the market for custom tees is surprisingly strong—in 2007, CafePress users sold over $100 million in T-shirts and other customizable merchandise.

Are T-shirts the answer for enhancing your company's revenue? Possibly not. But be bold and consider innovative outlets that enhance your brand image and profit line.

■ ■ ■

World War II brought additional business to P&G as the company's expertise was used to fill military contracts for 60-millimeter mortar shells. The company was a large producer of glycerin, used in explosives and medicines, which were vital in the war effort.

After World War II, new consumer attitudes demanded more products and P&G was ready for the challenge. The postwar period proved to be a spectacular growth period for the company, and one product in particular was a phenomenal success. Procter & Gamble had experimented with synthetic soaps and introduced Tide in 1946. The demand for this revolutionary soap outstripped production immediately as this product—along with a $21 million advertising campaign—was seen as a modern-day miracle. The product quickly became the most popular soap in America and has stayed that way for decades. Although the success of Tide was incredible, P&G continued to introduce new products, including Cheer, Downy, Bold, Era, and Solo.

With its flurry of successful products and market dominance, P&G's organic growth in the 1950s was unprecedented. In addition, the company hit on another incredibly successful innovation with the assistance of researchers at the University of Indiana. This time it was a unique toothpaste that included stannous fluoride. This combination of fluorine and tin that could significantly reduce cavities became known as Crest toothpaste. Introduced in 1955, this product rapidly became the number one selling toothpaste in America.

THE LESSON: THE POWER OF ACADEMIC COLLABORATION

It's one thing to collaborate with other businesses, even competitors, as Apple did with Microsoft under the guidance of Steve Jobs. It's quite another—as in, much safer—to collaborate with colleges and universities that nurture young, innovative minds as their primary purpose.

Many large businesses, especially those in the fields of biotechnology, medicine, and pharmaceuticals, collaborate with universities. Others focus on more general entrepreneurship, such as Washington University in St. Louis's Olin Cup. Every year, local businesses, students, and school alumni compete in an entrepreneurial event for a grand prize of $50,000 in seed money for their business. Programs like this promote innovation and give existing companies a chance to buy into innovation that complements or enhances their business strategy.

The next innovation horizon for Procter & Gamble was paper products, which also became popular in the 1950s. A new method of drying wood pulp led to several new products, including White Cloud, Puffs, and a reformulation for the famous Charmin brand.

■ ■ ■

But the best was yet to come. With the baby boom in full swing, the company introduced Pampers, which revolutionized the world of diapers. One of the company's researchers, Vic Mills, was changing one of his own grandchildren's leaking diapers one day when he decided that he could use his resources at P&G to do better (innovations truly come from tough times). Mills developed a three-layer paper diaper that absorbed moisture, kept it away from the baby's skin, and retained the fluid until the diaper was disposed of. This invention took the market by storm and has remained the standard of care for babies everywhere.

Over the years, P&G has acquired an array of companies so that it can stay in the forefront of consumer product innovation. It truly has created a culture that encourages, allows, and nurtures innovation. Procter & Gamble took a lucky situation with a floating bar of soap and turned it into gold. The power of luck is sometimes the result of people making mistakes. Patient innovators benefit from creating cultures where mistakes can happen. Few innovators are successful immediately, and many discover new ways of thinking simply by keeping an open mind to the opportunities that they might just stumble upon.

Chapter 11

GREED

Joe Cassano
AIG

This is a story of how an innovation was created to solve a problem. In that regard, the mission was accomplished. But the innovation was then used, without regard for ethics and morals, to amass great wealth, destroying a company and almost ruining the world's financial system.

This is a lesson of how even the most clever innovation can take a terrible turn for the worse, as I alluded to in the Introduction.

It reminds me of that famous Longfellow poem about a little girl, but with a terrible twist at the end. The poem, slightly altered, goes like this:

There was a little girl,
Who had a little curl,
Right in the middle of her forehead,
When she was good,
She was very good indeed,
But when *he* was bad *he* was horrid.

The little girl in our poem is Blythe Masters, who was the original creator of the credit default swap. It was created to innovatively service one of J.P. Morgan's large customers, Exxon. The man in the poem is Joe Cassano, the insurance magnate from AIG who directed his 400 employees to utilize this innovation in an unregulated environment to nearly sink the world economy.

The financial tsunami of 2008–2009 has produced all kinds of side effects that may qualify for the most maniacal mathematical exercises in financial history, including the subprime mortgage, auction rate preferred stock, and the asset-backed commercial paper. All are candidates for the most innovative weapon of mass financial destruction, but the credit default swap (CDS) is the granddaddy of greed.

We should have suspected that wolves were watching the chicken coop when the term *derivative* was invented and the layman was supposed to accept that these concoctions were just too complicated to understand. It is always a sure bet that when someone is taking something simple and making it complicated, they are planning to steal you blind. Such was the case of Joe the Insurance Man.

The credit default swap also stripped away the false face of the insurance industry by painfully demonstrating that the insurance industry is virtually the same thing as the gambling industry, except they don't serve free drinks and provide no headline entertainment. But I digress. Back to Joe the Insurance Man and AIG, the sponsor of my favorite soccer team.

Before we explore the rather simple innovation of a credit default swap, let's review the history of AIG.

AIG was founded by American Cornelius Vander Starr in 1919 in Shanghai, China. He was a pioneer as such, being the first westerner to sell insurance to the Chinese. He was quite successful until the new communistic regime asked him to leave in 1949.

He swiftly moved the company to New York City and was successful at expanding the firm through various subsidiaries into other markets including Latin America, Europe, and the Middle East.

In 1962, Starr hand-selected the next president of AIG, Maurice Greenberg, who dramatically changed the focus from personal insurance to higher-margin corporate insurance. He also changed the sales and distribution system to an independent agent system that would substantially reduce overhead. Eventually Greenberg succeeded Starr as the chairman and took the company public in 1968. During the next three decades, he led the company to become the largest insurance company in the world.

During Greenberg's reign, Joseph Cassano was recruited to AIG as the chief financial officer of the new financial product unit in 1987. By 1998, Cassano had discovered the innovation invented by Blythe Masters of J.P. Morgan that would make his career and destroy AIG. Back in those days it was called a *bistro*, but this was no French café.

The full name of this financial innovation was a *broad index secured trust offering*. Now that's a mouthful, and later the name would be refined to *credit default swap*—shorter, but still confusing. So what is this complex, fancy-schmancy, financial derivative thing anyway?

In late 1994, Blythe Masters, a rising star at J.P. Morgan, pitched an idea of selling the credit risk of a loan to Exxon through the European Bank of Reconstruction and Development (EBRD). The concept was simple: J.P. Morgan would sell the loan, but would guarantee EBRD a fee if the loan defaulted. In other words, EBRD was given an incentive/insurance to take on the loan. Bottom line, this financial maneuver satisfied all parties involved. It provided an innovative way to free up money for J.P. Morgan to invest in other more attractive projects, while keeping Exxon happy and giving EBRD financial motivation to take on the loan.

The credit default swap was useful, but it required a fair amount of effort with little incremental financial return specifically attached to the swap. However, a second invention would enable this financial maneuver to be exploited on the grand scale. This second invention was the creation of securitized debt. In simple terms, this is the grouping of loans into a package and selling them as a diversified package of debt. The theory is that some of the loans may be better than others, but the diversity of the package will in the end make it a viable investment. Simply put, this was a bet on the law of averages. The name given to this scheme was *collateral debt obligation* (CDO). However, the truly enabling component of this invention was that the banking industry then convinced ratings agencies like Moody's and S&P to give it the highest AAA rating—meaning it has close to zero credit risk.

As these packages became more varied in terms of risk, there was an obvious place in this equation for the concept of selling insurance to protect against the risk of bad debt. As securitized debts took on more risk, there was more reason for insurance. This makes perfect sense from a logical standpoint—*except* that insurance implies that the insurance company has the money in case the worst scenario happens.

As this innovation made its mark on Wall Street, Joe Cassano of AIG took a particular liking to this dubious derivative. The only problem is that he decided to exploit it without having the money to back up his risky behavior. The original innovator Masters was wary of this exploitation because the risks were not being engineered down to a safe level as had been the case in the Exxon transaction with J.P. Morgan.

As they say, the rest is history. Unfortunately, we are all paying for this history because *we* are the money that Joe Cassano and AIG used to cover their Vegas-style bets. Joe the Plumber had a difficult time paying his rent. Joe the Insurance Man is making it hard for America to pay its rent.

What he did was turn a sound financial innovation created by Blythe Masters into the world's largest collective bet to cover the housing boom, which was created by easy credit. He went on a horrid selling binge using the small but mighty 400-person office of AIG to sell a very new kind of insurance. Unlike traditional insurance, AIG didn't have to post any money up front. In other words, AIG could sell billions of dollars' worth of insurance to banks without having money for that rainy day. But that was only the tip of the iceberg because, in addition, this new insurance could be bought by a third party. In other words, you could place a bet with Joe the Insurance Man even if you didn't have a loan. This practice was called *naked* deals, and the sight of Joe the Insurance Man naked is not a pretty picture. It was pure speculation at this point, because the third-party buyers were betting on the outcome of loans of other parties. This was no different than betting on Manchester United to beat Chelsea in the Premier League.

And boy, could Joe bet. In the short span of seven years, he bet $500 billion worth of CDS protection, with at least $64 billion of that tied to the subprime mortgage market.

Like a Vegas hooker on his arm, AIG stood by and flashed its million-dollar smile and watched endearingly as the premiums kept rolling in. Unfortunately, AIG was enjoying the free cocktails so much that when it awakened from its night out on the town, it realized it had no money in its purse to cover Joe the Insurance Man's risky behavior.

Greed comes in all sizes, but you have to give Joe the Insurance Man credit—he didn't waste his time on small numbers. In 2005, Joe's efforts had produced $3.2 billion in revenue. Joe, like most high rollers, shared the winnings gratuitously with the 400 employees within his group. In all, over a seven-year period, Joe the Insurance Man made a tidy sum of $280 million (for himself), and his 400 friends were paid $3.5 billion.

Of course, innovations that are ruled by greed and regulated by no one come to an end. Joe was going to take down all the other people at the table, and some of those folks would get very angry.

By now we have forgotten that Uncle Sam sent a quick wire transfer of $180 *billion*. Now that is an expensive mistake to make from greed. And long after we move on to other difficulties, we will still be paying for this innovation being used without regard for rules and regulations, ethics and morals.

As an innovator, you have the choice of how you want to respond in the face of greed. When the world falls apart, do you throw a chair through a storefront window and start looting? Or do you make for higher ground and do the right thing?

We can all learn from the example of Robert Kearns, particularly the fact that taking the high road doesn't mean that you have to let people walk all over you.

You may have heard of Kearns through the movie *Flash of Genius*. He's the inventor of something we all take for granted today: the intermittent windshield wiper. Previously, windshield wipers didn't have settings or delays—they were simply on or off, and if they were on, they swiped furiously at the windshield, causing just as much distraction as the rain they were swiping away.

Kearns developed a prototype for the intermittent wiper and took it to the Ford engineers, who had been struggling to create an effective wiper of their own. They quickly decided that they liked what Kearns had put together, and Ford asked for pricing information and a sample model.

Then, suspiciously, Ford went silent. They wouldn't return Kearns' calls. After a while, the latest model of the Mustang was released, and guess what? Kearns's wipers were a featured improvement, with no credit, acknowledgment, or royalty to Kearns.

Ford got greedy, just like AIG. And they would suffer for it. Kearns tried to reason with Ford, to get what he was due, but they would hear none of it. They were a billion-dollar company, and he was just one man. So Kearns brought the matter to court. Refusing an early settlement, he eventually walked away with over $30 million in compensation for his revolutionary innovation. But more importantly for him, he walked away with the satisfaction that he had made the Ford Motor Company admit they had stolen the idea from an individual inventor.

Whether you're the little guy whose trust is abused or the big company who could get away with "borrowing" someone's innovation, you need to think about the long-term implications. Be a responsible innovator.

The simple reason for this chapter is to demonstrate that innovation is not intrinsically good or evil. Innovation can be used for good or evil, and therefore must be utilized with integrity.

Chapter 12

INTEGRITY

George Foreman
Salton Company

George Foreman has been my "Harvard case study" since I was 12 years old. In 1968, in a demonstration of patriotism, Foreman pulled out an American flag from his boxing boot after bringing home the gold medal in the Mexico Olympic Games. I was a young boy and I've never forgotten that moment. Here is what it meant to me: George Foreman, a black kid from Houston, was proud of his country, just like a white kid from St. Louis was proud of him. When he raised the American flag, instead of the then-fashionable black protest glove, he raised all of us to a higher level.

What does that have to do with innovation? Everything—everything that greed is not. I'm talking about integrity.

Fast-forward to 1994. My two oldest boys, twins Rob and Jon, are now 12 years old. We have watched every one of George Foreman's comeback fights and all of sudden, with one short, powerful punch, he knocks out Michael Moorer for the most stunning heavyweight victory in the history of boxing. As the boxing reverend

Foreman went to his corner, dropped to his knees, and said a prayer of thanksgiving, I thought to myself, this is divine providence. George Foreman has been my long-distance mentor for a long time, and now I have an opportunity to thank him, honor him, and, most importantly, expose his innovative genius.

The essence of George Foreman is integrity. His is not a persona that has been invented by a Madison Avenue public relations firm, but a real person that has survived a lifetime of experiences and shaped his future with the rock-solid principle of integrity.

Foreman grew up in the Fifth Ward of Houston, Texas, a place that won't be mistaken for Silicon Valley for its entrepreneurial environment. However, it has produced a brand of electrical grills that are the largest selling appliance in the history of the world.

Contrary to popular belief, Foreman didn't invent the grill. It was actually a man named Michael Boehm who found a way to allow grease to drain off a rather traditional appliance, a sandwich grill. George Foreman, however, was the true innovator, the reason why you and I know what a Foreman Grill is. He found a way to convince millions of people that this product was something that could improve their lives.

To call him a pitchman or salesman is to absolutely mischaracterize the genius of George Foreman. He is a brand, one that was established after his miraculous comeback in 1987. He is what companies spend millions of dollars trying to cultivate. But he did it with his own simple, profound logic. This logic was based on the principles of a God-centered life, which guided his actions as a boxer, businessman, and force for good in the world. He is the genuine article.

The Foreman Grill was simply the recipient of the power of integrity. It was the beneficiary of the honest effort of a man to restore himself financially so that he could continue to fund a youth center that he had started for underprivileged children and that was quickly running out of money. Boxing was his profession, and he had limited time to practice his skills before age would limit his ability to perform.

Many factors contribute and lead to the development of character. Character is the measure of integrity in a person, and in Foreman's case his character led him from the ghetto to glory to God. Innovation is not worth doing unless it has integrity, and George Foreman is a shining example of the power of integrity.

The Foreman Grill was innovative, but to say that it was revolutionary would be an overstatement. What made the difference is that it did what Foreman said it would do, and he was so forthright and compelling that we tried it . . . and liked it. Where did this passion come from and how did it happen?

The reason that Foreman had passion about it was because he wasn't just a salesman. He was a joint owner and he believed that he could convince others because he was genuinely convinced himself.

There is a huge lesson in innovation to be learned from this: Innovators must be convinced that what they are doing is worthwhile and works. This is what sustains the passion to pursue what appears to others to be either unimportant or even nonexistent. Also, an innovator must possess ownership of the idea in some form.

In all of the backgrounds of the innovators in this book, there was and is a belief that what they are doing is right and that it can work. As you or your company take on the new innovation age, one important principle that must never be overlooked is that innovation is very difficult. It is not an activity for the faint of heart. If you don't absolutely believe in what you're doing, there is a very high chance you will never succeed.

Take the example of Mark J. Manary, creator of Project Peanut Butter. Currently a researcher at Washington University, Manary has spent years cultivating an interest in and understanding of the widespread problem of child malnutrition in the third world. It's a problem so big that one man can't tackle it alone. Manary could have seen it that way and never tried. But he believed in his mission so much that he made the choice to try to make a difference, starting with just a few kids in Malawi.

Manary needed a relatively inexpensive, long-lasting, simple-to-produce, easy-to-transport substance to get in the hands of children. Peanut butter seemed like a perfect match, so after talking to a peanut butter developer in France, Manary concocted a similar substance that was enhanced with vitamins, minerals, sugar, and vegetable oil.

In the first two years of the project, 1,000 children in Malawi's largest hospital were enrolled. They were instructed to eat the peanut butter mixture three times a day for five weeks. They were also discharged from the hospital earlier than normal because Manary found that they recovered better at home.

The results were astounding. Because they finally had the vitamins and nutrients their young bodies needed, a full 95 percent of the children in the program fully recovered. They reached 100 percent of their ideal body weights for their heights, an important statistic for children who are usually underweight.

With dignity and integrity, Manary has started making an impact on the world. He believed he could make a difference. He started small, affecting the lives of 1,000 kids, but that number has grown to 7,000. With Project Peanut Butter achieving international praise and acclaim, his reach may soon grow far bigger than that.[1]

How does integrity affect the outcome of innovation? It is the intangible ingredient that keeps the innovator in the ring long enough to win the fight. Many times in my own career as an entrepreneur, I have reminded myself of the importance of staying in the ring long enough to weather the storm, always waiting for that knockout opportunity to break through to success.

George Foreman's return to boxing had two components that are essential for any innovator to embrace. First, he returned to the ring with a well-planned defense to allow him to pace himself through a fight. In other words, he didn't want to expend foolish energy, like he had against Muhammad Ali in the famous "Rumble in the Jungle" fight in 1974. Second, and most importantly, he punched with purity, not anger. This is a profound lesson for any innovator. You see, at one time in Foreman's career, he punched people to hurt them. In his comeback, he punched them to knock them out. I know this sounds a bit crazy, but follow me. A boxer's goal is to win the fight, not to hurt his opponent. It is much safer for someone to be temporarily knocked out than to absorb continuous punishment.

Foreman, an experienced boxer, realized the power he possessed in his punches and decided to use it professionally like a surgeon. If you are a boxing fan, you will find it interesting to watch his fights after he returned to the ring and witness this transformation.

The point is that innovation is very much a battle against the odds, and in order to succeed, innovators will benefit from three qualities that George Foreman possessed: a good defense, purity of intention, and perseverance with personality.

MODERN PARALLEL: TOM PHILLIPS, WEEKENDS ONLY

Tom Phillips entered the family business, a store in St. Louis called Phillips Furniture, in 1974. The concept of the store at the time was that the furniture pieces they contained were opportunity buys— pieces with dents and scratches. The showroom had no frills, and there were no options for customization. You took what you could get.

By 1984, the concept had evolved to higher-end furniture with sample rooms, brand names, and a polished showroom.

This worked fine for a while. But in 1992, Phillips noticed a downward trend at the store, which was in a lower-middle-class area of town. Over the next three years, revenue at that store steadily declined.

Phillips knew he had to make a change. With the guidance of some consultants, Phillips ran some studies to see what was working and what wasn't. He determined the following:

- Seventy percent of customer visits happened on the weekend.
- There wasn't adequate staff in the stores on the weekend.
- The most successful offerings were special sale events and opportunity buys.

So Phillips took the lead of a few other furniture stores around the country and completely retooled the concept of the company.

It now became Weekends Only: open Friday, Saturday, Sunday, and that's it.

The store embarked on an aggressive growth plan from 1997 to 2003. Weekends Only expanded to a total of six different locations with over 300 employees. Phillips installed complex traffic-monitoring software so he could constantly analyze the data to attain desired results.

Sales grew rapidly from around $1 million in 1997 to just over $30 million in 2004. But revenue plateaued, and again Phillips was left seeking answers.

You can build a company based on hard data, analytics, and logical thinking, but that will only take you so far. Phillips realized this. With the help of a local consultant group, CMA, Phillips decided to take a long, hard look at how his employees were feeling.

The results weren't good. Moral was low and yearly turnover was greater than 100 percent. Employees weren't feeling valued, and customers could sense it. So Phillips decided to focus on defining the mission and values of Weekends Only so they could be reflected in all aspects of the business, especially the employees.

The values Phillips outlined and focused on in later (and more frequent) communications with employees were responsibility, teamwork, performance, growth, honesty, and commitment. As Tom says, "I wanted more than good business results. I wanted committed, engaged associates working across departments, leveraging high-functioning relationships built on trust and respect."

Phillips isn't just saying this—he truly believes it. I've seen it in the way he treats anyone around him. He's an intense listener, he'll offer sound advice, and he believes in the power of appreciating employees. By embodying these traits, Phillips became, in essence, the chief *engagement* officer of Weekends Only.

Here are some of the ways that Phillips walks the walk:

- Creating a high-feedback environment: clear role definitions and expectations, performance accountability.
- Letting employees know that they matter and that they have the opportunity to grow and improve.

- Appreciating employees by giving family discounts and welcome/ birthday cards (all hand-signed by Phillips and the employee's supervisor).
- Celebrating and recognizing employees through an annual company picnic, annual recognition dinner and service awards, and pot-luck lunches.
- Community involvement: furnishing Habitat for Humanity homes.

Weekends Only is a testament of the power of creating a positive, engaging culture. After Phillips started incorporating these changes the revenue started to climb steadily. This growth has been sustained even through the 2008–2009 recession. That's the power of forming your company's culture with integrity. That's true innovation.

■ ■ ■

This chapter was almost called "The Power of Personality," but I chose "Integrity" instead because the essence of the likable George Foreman persona is that he is genuine to the bone. This is a very important part of true innovation. The nature of innovation is to develop many new ideas, and the ones that are pursued must be genuinely unique.

The success of the Foreman Grill is also a very good example of how innovations must have a complete fight plan. Just like Foreman's well-planned comeback in boxing, the Foreman Grill was a well-planned execution of an innovation program.

It started with the inventor, Michael Boehm, the unsung hero in the process. It was his key observation and invention that revealed a way to drain grease from the traditional cooking process. In some ways this is a very small difference, but certainly one that had great implications. His working name for the invention was the Short Order Grill. Not a bad name; in fact, I would say a very good name. But Michael, like a good boxing trainer, knew that it needed more to be successful in the rough-and-tumble market of the electrical appliance industry.

Michael Boehm is a savvy inventor because he knew the limitations of a great idea. This is a quality that few inventors possess. The innovator must make a disciplined decision in order to provide the idea a future, knowing that the formula for success will require additional talents and resources.

Michael Boehm understood the emotional side of inventions. First, he understood how to control his own emotions. It is difficult to share your idea when you know that your situation has limitations. It requires a sense of humility that is hard to harness when it's your idea. Second, and more importantly, he understood the need to tap into the emotion of the eventual market for his invention. This ability to understand the need for emotional engagement of his ideas with the end user was critical for the success of his product. Consequently, he realized that he needed somebody who could transform his idea into a real solution in the consumer world.

The kind of understanding exhibited by Boehm is a key ingredient in any innovation project. The development of an innovation team is critical because the innovation process requires a spectrum of skills, talents, and resources to be successful.

Just like the night Angelo Dundee was in George Foreman's corner when he regained his Heavyweight Champion of the World title, and the emotional attachment of Foreman wearing the same boxing shorts that he had worn 20 years previously in his loss to Muhammad Ali, innovation is an individual sport that nevertheless requires support from various people and must have an emotional element to provide the passion needed to attain success.

By the way, the George Foreman Grill has sold over 90 million grills since its inception, making it the most successful innovation ever in the appliance industry.

Chapter 13

THE INNOVATION GENERATION

The Internet has distributed information at less than wholesale cost, which has driven down the price of knowledge to commodity levels. It has provided a mechanism for anybody to research virtually any topic with a comfortable degree of certainty. The Internet has its shortcomings, but they are abundantly outweighed by the speed with which knowledge can be retrieved and disseminated.

This development has and will continue to have a significant impact on those industries that have long been dependent on keeping information as part of their business model (think Wikipedia vs. door-to-door encyclopedia salesmen of old). The cross-section of industries is vast and the power of the Internet is literally destroying certain sectors of industries at a precipitous rate.

This readily available knowledge and speed of communication is enabling a new breed of innovators with new resources that are forging the *innovation generation*.

The innovation generation is more of an evolution than a revolution. Although the impact may ultimately be greater than that of the industrial revolution, it is a very organic transition from the ease with which information can be collected, using the power of creative assimilation and entrepreneurial ingenuity.

Much has been written about a shift from left-brain thinking (the analytical types) to right-brain thinking (the creative types), but the innovation generation will be the epiphany of *balanced brain* thinkers, those who can strike a balance between analytical and creative skills. In an economy that is changing daily, many of the old management and organizational paradigms are too cumbersome to meet the fast-paced decisions and actions that will have to be taken to compete.

For example, in offices of yore, most employees had a single, small computer monitor. Even up to the mid-2000s, 17-inch monitors were the norm. Now you walk through an office and you see huge monitors on each desk, sometimes even two monitors. This may seem like excessive technology, but really it's just a sign of the sheer number of tasks, duties, and information that any employee must juggle to maintain maximum efficiency.

This trend will continue. Although the two-monitor solution may seem over the top, research shows that having two monitors actually increases productivity by 44 percent.[1] Think about it: You have your multitabbed Web browser open on one monitor and your active program—word processor, spreadsheet, client database—on the other. Instead of clicking back and forth between separate windows, your eyes can flick between the two monitors (which is *much* faster than the speed of your hand on the mouse). Our brains are being conditioned to handle massive amounts of information in bite-sized quantities, so why not match your employees' technology with their mental capacity?

Sooner than later, multitasking will be replaced with multi-skills. Some specialized information will remain a key part of the economy, but if your specialty is based on a collection of semiprivate information, you will be competing with the quickly improving search engines of the Internet. With the vast amount of information out there, if you can't search for something, you're probably not going to find it.

Multi-skills and versatile problem-solving abilities will provide the supple, symphonic thinking model that will empower individuals to see the broad strokes of change within their internal and external environments.

Risk taking will come back in style, but with a more disciplined approach. The world economic recession has affected enough people in a negative manner that it has consequently taught all classes of investors a lesson regarding the need for both calculated risks and veracity of information.

What skill sets will serve you well? There are four basic and simple skills that are critical to competing in the innovation generation: untying knots, illustrative communication, connecting dots, and simplifying complexities.

UNTYING KNOTS

Many people are great at tying knots, but few have the aptitude to untie them. This is part skill and part patience. In many ways it is reverse vision. To understand how a knot got to its current state and then reengineer it to untie it takes a flexible mind. Likewise, many problems of the future will be a simple reengineering of past work. For example, there is much activity in the field of biomimicry. In simple terms, we are trying to reengineer life in a synthetic way, which nature has done for centuries.

The essence of intuitive thinking is simply rethinking how something is done in a more natural progression. This is why Apple continues to innovate and improve the operation of their various devices.

Adam Boesel had a big knot to untie. Basically, he wanted to start a gym. But starting a gym is not such a basic idea. There are hundreds of different types of gyms out there—how could he create one that differentiated itself from the others?

Boesel decided to focus on the "green" concept. Green makes for good marketing and good press. So he started researching how he could create a green gym, and he found a gym in Hong Kong that was experimenting with ways to generate electricity.

So Boesel connected a small generator to a spin bike. By pedaling on the bike, he generated small amounts of electricity.

Soon after, Boesel moved to Portland, an environmentally progressive city, and opened the Green Microgym. His idea had become a reality. Now he just needed people to find out about it.

ILLUSTRATIVE COMMUNICATION

Communication seems like an obvious skill, but as the information age unfolded, an ironic outcome began to develop. The more technology we have to communicate, the less we develop the actual *skills* to communicate. This has caused a dearth of capable communicators, which is one of the most important assets of the innovation generation.

Conceptual communication will play a vital role in advancing innovation. Ideas come from people, and people transform ideas into reality. If they lack the ability to effectively explain their concepts, these ideas will never reach reality.

Boesel created a concept that stuck in people's minds. As soon as they heard about the gym where you could generate the electricity for the lights above, they had to share it with someone else.

Soon the local media caught on to the idea, as did bloggers across America. That's how I heard about it—I saw a link on a random blog to a cool concept someone was trying out in Portland. People hear about the gym where exercise machines generate electricity, and the idea resonates in them because it seems like such an obvious and clever pairing of two technologies.

CONNECTING THE DOTS

Connecting the dots is another way of seeing the big picture. In a fast-paced economy, outcome thinking is necessary to integrate the rapid development of products, processes, and relationships.

Big-picture thinking must be balanced with small actions. No matter how big the picture, it is the small things that make the difference.

These two skill sets have traditionally been seen as polar opposites. But in the innovation generation, the ability to balance the two will be the key factor to success.

Despite the brilliant concept and positive press, the Green Microgym didn't make a profit until the last quarter of 2009. The problem was that it opened its doors at the beginning of the 2008–2009 recession, a time when people were cutting discretionary spending, not adding it.

Boesel could have closed up shop, perhaps waited for a better time to reopen, but instead he pursued his dream despite the economy. The key for his success was that he paid attention to his clients and connected the dots as he became more aware of what attracted people to the gym.

In the beginning, two bikes were retrofitted with the generator technology. The problem was that they were really loud. Not many people were using them. Without those bikes, his gym was no different than other gyms.

Boesel realized that he needed to incentivize customers to use the generator bikes. So he created the "Burn and Earn" program. However, if you do the math, 20 hours of pedaling on one of those bikes translates to about one kilowatt hour, which generates about $0.15 of electricity. That's not much of an incentive for someone to use one of the bikes.

So Boesel decided to offer $1 in local restaurant gift certificates (collectible in $10 increments) for every hour of electricity produced. Although bike users weren't creating a dollar's worth of electricity, Boesel didn't lose any cash because the gift certificates were donated. Nonetheless, people felt like they were getting a good deal, helping the environment, and earning bragging rights for the electricity they generated, so everyone wins. Generator bike use jumped, and soon the gym had a growing cadre of members.

SIMPLIFYING COMPLEXITIES

Great innovators have always understood the importance of simplifying complexities. Now, there is an even greater sense of urgency to capture the essence of subjects. As science pushes toward understanding our genetic makeup to solve health problems, we see a glowing example of the necessity to peel back the layers of complexity to understand the simplest form of life.

Simplicity is very closely related to intuitiveness. It is understanding life as the essence of human behavior that drives great innovation. This is why innovation is powered by the many human qualities that have been outlined in this book.

The Green Microgym started with two clunky, loud, electricity-generating bikes. It seems simple enough, but really the technology itself needed to be streamlined.

Boesel has made it his personal and professional goal to have as many quiet, electricity-generating bikes in the gym as possible. In a relatively short time, he has retrofitted six bikes with a more advanced technology, along with four elliptical trainers and one treadmill. He's also upgraded other machines to technology that uses less electricity, including two elliptical machines that are completely self-generating. And he installed solar panels on top of the gym.

In some ways, Boesel is adding to the complexity of his gym. But in others, he's continually driving the gym to meet all the hype it originally generated. As the gym becomes more energy efficient and the membership increases, he'll rely less and less on the power grid. And he'll be able to franchise the idea out to entrepreneurs in other areas of the country, spreading this novel concept. But he'll always remain the true original.

■ ■ ■

These are the basic qualities that the innovation generation will need to embrace in order to compete in the kaleidoscopic culture and ephemeral economy that will continue to evolve faster each decade.

Chapter 14

THE SANDBOX UNIVERSE

When I was kid, I would get on my bike, ride to my friend's house, and literally call his name in an elevated voice to persuade him to come out and play ball. It was along the lines of, "Ohhhhhhh Frank!" I didn't use the telephone to call ahead or the doorbell once I reached his house. We would play basketball or baseball on his driveway and pretend we were some of our favorite players. That was 1967.

Today, my youngest son, Luke, turns on the PS3 and plays with some fast friend in Japan in a virtual battle to save the universe. The premise is the same, but the sandbox just got a little bigger.

We are beyond being global. That's a twentieth-century term used for companies that would build a plant or office in a faraway land. The difference today is that we can literally be in two places at one time. In other words, the collaborative sandbox reaches around the world and around the clock. Communication technology has made it possible not only to tear down barriers, but to make walls and fences irrelevant.

This incredible leap in communicative power brings with it the need for a construct to give order to the new world of innovation.

Innovation will be a part of every organization in the twenty-first century. The rate of change in every industry is increasing so rapidly that managing the impact of innovation is no longer just an issue for technology companies that must introduce new versions of products each year.

In the innovation generation, we will live in a sandbox universe. We are light-years past global—we are now universal. From the comfort of your living room and a smart-phone, we now can interact with our friends anywhere in the world on many different dimensions. Change is now a constant because information barriers have been eliminated. Now with a simple click of the mouse, many businesses have been replaced with online versions.

The innovation generation will be ruled by those with a flexible skill set and a curious mind. No longer will entire professions be protected by exclusivity of knowledge. The curious mind will be able to penetrate almost instantly into any field imaginable, and the result will be new methods to accomplish old tasks that will make past practices obsolete almost instantly.

Every business, university, or organization should embrace the innovation generation as the new platform of competitive existence. This new age of change is something not to be feared but to be embraced because of two fundamental reasons. First, the existing and the developing technologies will not slow down; they will continue indefinitely. There is no turning back. Second, this era will create new opportunities for an entirely new generation of thinkers and doers. No longer will monopolistic thought or protected information be a guarantee of success or security.

The businesses, universities, and organizations that can get comfortable with change will flourish. Those that cannot will soon find that they will become extinct. This phenomenon will sweep through virtually every industry in the world and the impact will be profound.

How do people and organizations get comfortable with change, if in fact it is not part of their corporate or personal DNA? By following a simple construct to create an environment that encourages, promotes, and facilitates innovation.

This construct is called the *sandbox universe*. In the following pages I explore this construct, ending with some news about a leading university, and illustrate how the construct can benefit you and your organization. The sandbox universe construct provides guideposts to encourage innovation, but also guidelines to manage it once it occurs. Innovation isn't a new thing—it's been around since the beginning of time. But because the barriers to change have been torn down in recent decades, innovation has been liberated to run like the wind.

Remember when we were proud of American ingenuity? Well, get ready for an encore. Now, the stakes are even higher than before. America, because of its superior university system, entrepreneurial heritage, and freedom to allow new ideas to flourish is perfectly positioned to continue its leadership in innovation.

All the ingredients are in place to make true again the words of Thomas Payne in 1776, "We have it in our power to begin the world over again." But actions always speak louder than words, and that is why the sight of George Foreman taking the American flag from his boxing shoe and raising it to demonstrate to the world that the United States is the leader of the free world is my personal favorite mental image of the innovation generation.

This time, the new beginning will occur through collaboration between businesses, universities, and individual innovators. The sandbox universe provides a simple foundation for this activity to be nurtured in your organization. Read on and soon you will be well equipped to inspire imagination that can be harnessed to create great things for the world.

First, a mental picture is helpful to provide the image and the relationships within the sandbox universe construct. The sandbox universe has four sides, each representing a foundational attribute. The four sides represent inspiration, imagination, innovation development, and industrialization. The center of the box represents integrity, which has a direct relation to each of the four sides.

INTEGRITY

The sandbox universe must be anchored at its core with integrity. This is the structural system in the foundation of innovation. Every aspect of innovation must comply with the standards of excellence and ethics. Without this backbone, innovation can and will be a destructive force in any organization. Innovation by its nature requires the collaboration and cooperation of many different parties. Without standards of excellence and ethics, these collaborations will break down quickly when strain is placed on the relationships.

As businesses, universities, and organizations of all types begin to embrace the integration of innovation as a key strategic element of their operations, it is imperative that establishing standards of excellence and ethics precedes any other development activity.

INSPIRATION

Inspiration is the source of innovation. The archaic meaning of *inspiration* is to "breathe life into." Many books have been written to help motivate people to lose weight, to speak in public, and to overcome various challenges in their lives. Motivation is a necessary ingredient in pursuing any endeavor, but inspiration has a more powerful and longer-lasting effect. Its transforming effect is permanent.

Where does inspiration come from? Now that is a question with a million answers, but let me identify two of the enabling sources of this powerful force.

Because inspiration is permanent, most sources of inspiration generally come from images that last in perpetuity even if it is only the fond memory of a loved one. By contrast, motivation generally comes from words of encouragement, but as those words subside, the motivation does as well.

Many of the great innovators have found their inspiration in fulfilling a promise to someone. I know that I promised my own kids that I would be the pioneer of my family who tried to become an entrepreneur, because I felt that I owed it to my own father, who desperately wanted to but did not have the opportunity. I also felt responsible to fulfill this obligation so that my kids could learn from my mistakes.

Of course, each person will have their own source of inspiration, but the key is to replenish your inspiration from the same fount which it originally sprang. To this day, I look at my Dad's watch from Western Union and remind myself that he showed me the way. I look at the faces of my wife and children and remember the promise I made to them.

As we transition from the information age to the innovation generation, a new standard of competition will be essential to ensure success in a universal marketplace where barriers will be replaced with brain power. Inspecting the files of the U.S. Patent Office yields a simple conclusion: Innovation is the result of individuals, not institutions who have been inspired to solve a problem. Respect for the individual mind is an essential component in this new age. Collective thought and teamwork can build businesses to take advantage of these innovations, but individual thought is the essential game changer.

IMAGINATION

Imagination is a powerful yet fragile talent that must be encouraged and nurtured if innovation is going to occur. The proper allotment of time, incentives, and support must be given to individuals in organizations if they are going to generate ideas. Each entity will have its own unique ways to encourage the culture of imagination, but one thing is certain: Imagination must be embraced from the top down, whether the company is a university, a large corporation, a small business, or a nonprofit.

How does an organization nurture imagination?

Here are four core guidelines for nurturing imagination. They are by no means designed to be exhaustive, but hopefully helpful:

1. *Fair financial/nonfinancial incentives*—this one should top the list.
2. *Personal recognition* among colleagues and superiors.
3. *Freedom* and *designated time and space* allowed.
4. *Guidance and expertise* to assist in the innovative development of ideas.

These should be the minimum support parameters provided to nurture imagination in your organization. Imagination is a talent that must be identified. It cannot be arbitrarily instituted, but must have room to bloom. The results usually are not immediate, and many innovations take a while to reach the market and/or will be modified many times before they are ready for prime time. In essence, leadership in any organization that embraces imagination must also have patience to let innovation grow or it is not worth pursuing.

INNOVATION DEVELOPMENT

Innovation development starts with an idea. This idea must then be fully conceptualized and somehow demonstrated by either a drawing, a model, or some other form of illustration so that it can be presented to a lawyer or patent agent. Your idea may fall under one of three major intellectual property categories: patents, trademarks, or copyrights.

A *patent* is only for inventions in machines, methods, manufactures, compositions of matter, designs, and asexually produced plants. An invention, to be patentable, must be novel, useful, and nonobvious. The requirement of novelty means that something new is disclosed. Novelty exists if the invention has not been described in a publication or patent anywhere in the world, or if there has been no prior public use or sale in this country. The requirement of utility means the performance of some beneficial function, even if only crudely. The requirement that it be nonobvious means that the subject matter would not be obvious to a skilled worker if he had available to him all prior knowledge. All three requirements are essential, and all three must coexist.

A *trademark* is a distinctive sign or indicator used by an individual, business organization, or other legal entity to identify that the products or services with which the trademark appears originate from a unique source, and to distinguish its products or services from those of other entities.

A *copyright* is a form of intellectual property that gives the author of an original work exclusive rights for a certain time period in relation to that work, including its publication, distribution, and adaptation, after which time the work is said to enter the public domain. Copyright applies to any expressible form of an idea or information that is substantive and discrete and fixed in a medium.

Of course, there is a cost to protect your ideas via these forms of intellectual properties. Patent are the most expensive and easily run in the range of $5,000 to $10,000 and even higher, depending on the patent and the geographical reach of the protection. Trademarks are much less expensive and usually range from $500 to $1,500. This number can also increase substantially if the product or service is intended to be used outside the United States. And finally, copyrights are the least expensive and are virtually free for most uses.

Creation and protection of an idea are the foundational aspects of innovation, but many patents today are still collecting dust in the patent office, waiting for someone to commercialize these ideas and successfully bring them to market.

INDUSTRIALIZATION

As demonstrated in the examples in this book, there are many different configurations for commercializing good ideas. However, it is safe to say that the options for commercialization fall under three major categories: licensing, start-up, and corporate.

LICENSING

Licensing simply refers to leveraging the innovation—or, to use the more specific term, the intellectual property—via a second party who would acquire the rights to use the innovation in some form and then return a financial compensation to the inventor. This format is very common for universities and individuals who do not have the resources or the expertise to build a company to bring the innovation to market.

This avenue offers many benefits to the innovator regarding reducing risk and exposure. In essence, the product development, marketing, and financing functions are taken on by the potential licensee. In return the licensee will potentially reap the larger financial gain, but they also carry the development risk.

Examples in this book include the Super Soaker and the George Foreman Grill.

START-UP

Some innovators choose to build a company around their innovation. This of course requires completely different skill sets, including entrepreneurial development and business management skills.

The risks are very high, but the returns are also potentially enormous. Most companies featured in this book fall into this category, such as Apple, Hersheys, Procter & Gamble, Johnson & Johnson, and so forth.

CORPORATE

Many companies that exist today can benefit by implementing a sandbox universe construct to fortify their competiveness for the future. In essence, all companies must at least conceptually adopt a sandbox construct, even if they do not have resources to formally staff a department or a division. The key is to create a culture of innovation in an organization so as to be aware and encourage their personnel to exercise their minds and to stretch horizons. In addition, personnel who participate in this culture must be fairly rewarded for their efforts. The days of handing over all your thoughts for free to the corporation will soon be gone.

Of course, it is critical for companies to be able to evaluate and act on the innovation that occurs. Small corporate staffs can benefit enormously from the facilitation of innovation, while using outside law firms on an as-needed basis.

The bottom line is that all industries of tomorrow will change so rapidly that any company not embracing a culture of innovation will be severely handicapped for long-term success. The rate of change in industry-leading companies in today's innovative environment makes leadership positions incredibly tenuous, and they will get even more vulnerable as the information age gives way to the innovation generation.

THE SANDBOX UNIVERSE AT ST. LOUIS UNIVERSITY: A CASE STUDY

To demonstrate how this construct can help your organization, I thought it would be helpful to show you how we use it at St. Louis University. First, we have an office dedicated to innovation. We call it the Office of Innovation and Intellectual Property. We see our role as a service to the university that inspires, protects, and facilitates our faculty, students, and staff to innovate in order to provide the world with better solutions. We have a small staff of three people and we utilize outside legal counsel in matters of patents, trademarks, and copyrights.

We have various *sandboxes* (intellectual property projects) in our innovation portfolio, ranging from medicines to medical instruments to aviation technologies to the arts. In simple terms, if a member of the university community submits a patentable idea, the university funds that patent expense, commercializes the patent, and shares the royalty revenue stream with the inventor. The inventor's share is 40 percent of the royalties collected. In simple terms, the innovators are owners and have a very attractive incentive to discover the next idea. Your organization may use a different incentive program—ours is by no means the only way—but it is critical that the innovators share as an equity partner in their ideas.

The following is an example of how our system works and how you can utilize the sandbox universe for your organization.

We have a rather exciting sandbox, or project portfolio, that we call the *sustainable sandbox*. These are projects that address creating or enhancing energy efficiencies. Currently, our sustainable sandbox contains several very exciting projects, and I share one here to demonstrate how the sandbox universe construct is used to facilitate the growth of innovation. The project is called Quantum Weather.

INSPIRATION

A light bulb went *off* in my head!

Usually, it's the other way around when it comes to innovation, but for two researchers at St. Louis University, it was the loss of electricity that inspired them to solve a problem.

Dr. Robert Paskin and Dr. William Dannevik, members of the Department of Earth and Atmospheric Sciences, were both victims of severe power outages in the St. Louis area in 2006. The loss of electricity was due to two devastating storms that left in their wake the largest power outages in the history of St. Louis.

Dannevik had previously done research at the University of California's Lawrence Liverpool laboratory and had explored the possibility of developing a "virtual valley" of weather prediction models for California's rapidly developing Central Valley. Paskin was watching both storms on radar and realized that with advanced forecasting models, computer-aided information, and a network of weather reporting, he could develop a system that predicted atmospheric conditions much more precisely.

IMAGINATION

Paskin and Dannevick refer to their innovation as "neighborhood weather" because they imagined predicting weather down to the street level. I remember as a kid being amazed at how on a hot summer day, one side of my street could have rain falling and the other side was bone dry. Now, I had met the scientists who could tell when that was going to happen.

What this meant from an electricity perspective was that if "neighborhood weather" was indeed possible, then the electric company would have a very specific advanced warning system to protect or repair electrical lines when a storm was passing through the area. Sounds good in theory, but will anybody believe this? How many times does the TV weather person get the weather wrong? And now these two scientists think they can predict weather down to the street level 12 hours before the storms arrive?

Dannevick and Paskin was now faced with the business of selling Imagination—a job thought to be reserved for the likes of Walt Disney or Steve Jobs. But throwing fear to wind (so to speak), they arranged a meeting with AmerenUE, the supplier of the area's electricity.

To their pleasant surprise, Dave Wakeman, AmerenUE's vice president responsible for power distribution and repairing the power lines damaged by storms, was more than intrigued. In fact, he was willing to invest in time and equipment for Dannevick and Paskin to achieve their neighborhood weather goal.

INNOVATION DEVELOPMENT

Over the next two years, Dannevick and Paskin, in partnership with Dave Wakeman and AmerenUE, developed an intricate process and system that would receive, evaluate, and forecast with amazing accuracy from perpetual information retrieved from strategically placed weather-reporting units high atop the AmerenUE electrical poles.

Now, as the patent process cures and continued refinement is being done to broaden the use of the technology, SLU and AmerenUE continue to develop a local model that has already saved AmerenUE substantial financial and human resources, but more importantly has drastically improved the preparedness and repair times, which has kept the lights on in St. Louis.

This partnership is a modern-day example of how in the innovation generation, universities and industry will collaborate to bring cutting-edge innovation to market. This university-industry model is an underutilized asset in the United States and can be the ultimate competitive edge in the universal marketplace of ideas.

INDUSTRIALIZATION

As this sustainable sandbox emerges onto the marketplace, it is now ready to begin its ascent into the universe. With lofty goals and objectives, the project once known as "neighborhood weather" has been given a new trademark, Quantum Weather™, to better communicate the size and scope of the potential impact of the project. In 2010, the expansion of the program will begin to provide a patented national weather system that can be used for commercial, homeland security, and sustainability projects and will redefine the forecasting of weather.

An imaginary idea, an investment partner, a patented process, and a purpose with integrity make for great innovation. Stay tuned . . .

EPILOGUE

The Power of the Bayh-Dole Act

Most Americans have never heard of the Bayh-Dole Act. But all Americans benefit from the results of this landmark legislation. It has changed the face of Innovation in America and has established a foundation by which to more fully harness the power of American Ingenuity.

The Bayh-Dole Act will celebrate its thirtieth birthday this year. I could have called it an anniversary, but it is really a birthday because being thirty is young, celebrating a thirtieth anniversary connotes well, middle age. I know, our thirtieth wedding anniversary is next year.

The Bayh-Dole Act is the most important piece of legislation in American Innovation History. This act, which was written by Senator Birch Bayh and Senator Robert Dole unleashed the power of American Intellectual Ingenuity and Free Enterprise.

For those who are not familiar, this act allowed Universities to monetize discoveries that were made from publicly funded research.

Before this act, all inventions that were discovered by university researchers via government grants were the property of the government. This has two inherent problems: First, since it is owned by the public, anyone and everyone can use it. On face value this might seem like good thing, except that the reality is very few companies are willing to invest in technology that anybody can use. Second, the government did not have the skills or interest in learning how to commercialize these nonexclusive technologies.

I began my career in Innovation Management the same year, 1980, and I can recall how the naysayers in the world were writing off America Ingenuity and Competiveness as a fading picture of the past. Of course, looking back, this was the beginning of the largest technology boom in our history, thanks in large measure to the Bayh–Dole Act.

The United States Research Universities are the envy of the world. They make up the overwhelming majority of leading research institutions and are the largest investment in innovation in the world.

The results of Bayh-Dole Act are incredibly impressive considering that this was a new development in 1980, which would take time and a considerable transformation of culture on the part of universities and industry to understand and then gear up to transfer these inventions to market.

To briefly touch on the success of the Bayh-Dole Act, according to the 2006 Survey of AUTM (Association of University Technology Managers) consider that in only 30 years:

- More than 6,000 new U.S. companies were formed from university inventions.
- Two new companies were formed every working day of the year;
- There were 4,350 new products that came on the market as a result of Bayh-Dole.
- 5,000 active university–industry licenses are in effect, mostly with small companies.

A study supported by the Biotechnology Industry Organization (BIO) on the impact of university patent licensing on the U.S. economy between 1996 and 2007 has just been released. Even using very conservative methodologies, that study reports:

- $187 billion impact on the U.S. gross domestic product
- $457 billion impact on U.S. gross industrial output
- 279,000 new jobs created in the United States from university inventions

A 2009 survey of BIO member companies reveals how dependent that the Bio industry is on patent licensing, largely from universities, finding that:

Fifty percent of those reporting said their companies were based on in-licensed technologies; and 76 percent have licensing agreements with U.S. universities in place.

Recently, the Bayh-Dole Act has come under attack from a couple of unusual sources. The Kaufman Foundation and the Harvard Business Review have co-promoted a "solution" of dismantling the system and letting individual inventors, instead of their sponsoring universities, undertake the formidable task of investing in and managing the patenting process and the even more tenuous process of innovation development.

Although this suggested solution is woefully naive of the comprehensive process, and need for proper alignment of universities, inventors, industry and U.S. tax payers, it does provide an opportunity for those of us who have participated in the first 30 years to rededicate ourselves to pioneer new and more effective standards of practice for this young adventure.

Instead of dismantling a relatively young system, universities and industry needs to be forging new ways to work together in order to create a new American Innovation Revolution.

Just as universities have gone through and are still going through a transformation of learning how to transfer intellectual assets to industry, industry is also learning new ways to interact with universities.

So how do we take Bayh-Dole to the next level? Before I proceed, let me thank Senators Bayh and Dole on their pioneering work in innovation and I would suggest to them that Innovators never get old, they just reinvent themselves.

Here are my suggestions:

- Universities should place a higher priority on creating a culture of innovation.
- Universities should increase their innovation education to students and researchers.
- Innovation Management Offices should be organized and managed like a business, positioning the office to be an efficient and effective gateway between industry and the university.
- Industry should view universities as full partners in research, including equitable intellectual property policies that protect the expertise of university scientists.
- Industry should help promote the culture of innovation by sponsoring innovation education and contests with universities.

The bottom line is that there is so much underutilized potential that still exists because of the relatively short time the Bayh–Dole Act has been in existence and this recession is a perfect time for universities and industries to forge stronger and more innovative ways to create more commercial power from this endless resource that is unique to America.

NOTES

Chapter 2 Perseverance: Thomas A. Edison, General Electric Company

1. http://edison.rutgers.edu/biogrphy.htm.

Chapter 3 Pain: Walt Disney, Laugh-O-Gram Films

1. Neal Gabler, *Walt Disney: The Triumph of American Imagination* (Random House, 2007).
2. www.infinitypoint0.com/60/imdb-film-length-project/
3. Perry Romanowski, "Electronic Ink,"*How Products Are Made* 6, www.madehow.com/Volume-6/Electronic-Ink.html.

Chapter 4 Intuition: Steve Jobs, Apple Inc.

1. Chuck Salter, "The Most Valuable Player in Sports Is This Doctor," *Fast Company*, no. 128 (September 2008), www.fastcompany.com/magazine/128/the-most-valuable-player-in-sports-is-this-doctor.html.
2. http://developer.apple.com/adcnews/pastissues/devnews121997.html#stats.
3. Forrester Research, "U.S. E-commerce Forecast: 2008 to 2012," referenced in Linda Rosencrance, "E-commerce Sales to Boom for Next 5 Years," *Computerworld Networking*, February 5, 2008, www.computerworld.com/s/article/9061108/E_commerce_sales_to_boom_for_next_5_years_.

Chapter 5 Simplicity: Robert W. Johnson, Johnson & Johnson

1. www.fundinguniverse.com/company-histories/Johnson-amp;-Johnson-Company-History.html

2. Deborah Netburn, "The Taste That Launched 1,000 Parking Tickets," *L.A. Times*. August 4, 2006, http://www.latimes.com/business/la-et-pinkberryaug04,0,5813232.story.

3. John Kranz, "The Flip Takes 13% of the Camcorder Market by Doing Less," *Signal vs. Noise* blog, http://37signals.com/svn/posts/923-the-flip-takes-13-of-the-camcorder-market-by-doing-less.

Chapter 12 Integrity: George Foreman, Salton Company

1. Diane Duke Williams, "Peanut Butter Progress," Newsroom, Washington University in St. Louis, http://news.wustl.edu/news/Pages/2708.aspx

Chapter 13 The Innovation Generation

1. Christopher Null, "Two Monitors = 44 Percent Increase in Productivity," Yahoo! Tech, January 16, 2009, http://tech.yahoo.com/blogs/null/115846?comment_start=6&comment_ count=20.

ABOUT THE AUTHOR

Thomas A. Meyer, MBA, CLP, is the Chief Innovation Officer of St. Louis University. Meyer's career in Innovation Management spans more than 30 years. He created the Domestic and International Intellectual Property Office at Anheuser-Busch, Inc. in 1980. He co-authored the pioneering book on Intellectual Property Management in 1988, *An Executive's Complete Guide to Licensing.* For more than 20 years, Meyer has consulted many Fortune 500 and privately owned companies in the areas of licensing, franchising, new product development, and marketing. A partial list of clients includes Coca-Cola, Times Mirror Corporation, Ralston Purina, and CBS Radio and TV.

Meyer is also an accomplished entrepreneur who has founded four successful companies in the manufacturing, retail, and services industries. He has been responsible for developing some of the first sustainable products including the first 100-percent recycled plastic bottle in 1991 and the first bio-based automotive commodity chemicals in 1994. Meyer's new professional passion is building bridges between industry and universities to ensure America's Innovation Leadership in the World.

INDEX